CONTENTS

INTRODUCTION TO THE BOOK OF JAMES

The Book of James is one of the most remarkable books of the Bible. It has endured more criticism and misunderstanding than any other book in the New Testament. As far as we know, it wasn't until about A.D. 200 that the Book of James was recognized as Scripture. At that time Origen quoted James on an equal footing with other portions of the Bible. Luther, the great Protestant reformer, never did accept James's letter because of its seeming contradiction to Paul's doctrine of justification by faith. Luther's attitude was unwarranted and has done a great disservice to the purpose and effectiveness of the book. In spite of the slow acceptance by the church, in addition to the book's controversial nature, the Book of James has come to be recognized as not only an authentic New Testament document, but also a book with an essential message to every generation. The church has needed this message to keep from straying toward a preoccupation with mysticism, or with noncommittal faith that has no practical outworking in daily life.

James is a contemporary book because the forcefulness and succinctness of its message speak directly to man's needs and condition. One reason Luther did not like the Book of James was that it did not have the theological particulars logically defined as a basis for its teaching. James breaks right in and gets to the heart of his subject in practical terms. Paul usually set the stage for his teaching by presenting a theological basis for faith and then used the latter part of his letters to give practical rules of conduct. There's really no contradiction between Paul and James because Paul also believed in practicality, right conduct, and even in "good works" (Eph. 2:10). However, in his letter James does not give a theological basis; he gets right into practical concerns and makes his point clear and concise.

James is much like the writers of Proverbs, Ecclesiastes, and Hebrew wisdom literature. He writes with conciseness and brevity, he capsulates truth, and makes his point with simplicity and forcefulness. He uses comparison and contrast much like the Hebrew poets. He likes to jolt people out of their lethargy and start them thinking about what they say they believe. For James, one of the greatest sins is to separate one's ethics from one's theology, to assume that one can have right doctrine but not care about how he lives. The greatest heresy is hypocrisy. For he who "knows what is right to do and fails to do it, for him it is sin" (James 4:17).

James makes no attempt to give explanations. He says just what he means, quickly and precisely. He says to count it joy when you meet trouble (1:2); if you lack wisdom, ask God (1:5); don't blame God for temptation (1:13); practice what you preach (1:22); partiality is sin (2:1); faith without works is dead (2:17); the tongue is

6

nasty (3:6); strife is caused by evil passions (4:1, 2); life is short (4:14); the rich are miserable (5:1). These are samples of the range of subjects James treats.

James starts from the assumption that what he says is true. To live right before God and man is one of the best evidences that a person's faith is genuine and is grounded in truth. While not going as far as modern pragmatists, we could say that James teaches that *truth is practice;* that is, if one possesses truth and it grips him in his innermost being, it will then work itself out in practical action. This is in keeping with James's basic theme. Faith in the Lord Jesus Christ must be applied to every aspect and relationship of life. Faith cannot hide behind a believism that emphasizes only creed and not deed. For James, it is conduct that proves creed. A good creed does not guarantee good conduct.

One of the failures of the contemporary evangelical church has been at this point. By being on the defensive and avoiding contact with those in error, the church repudiated many of the essential elements of true evangelicalism. Social concern and good works were looked upon with suspicion. Taboos about dress and entertainment became primary, and correct doctrine a fetish. The relationship between right doctrine and ethical living was blurred in a storm of controversy over much that was nonessential.

Not all evangelicals fell into this trap, but many did and still do limit themselves to a Christianity that aligns itself with partisan politics, pseudopatriotism, and a shallow, antiquated evangelism. The question that arises is whether such faith is really true faith. In the light of a serious study of the Book of James, there is doubt about the reality of religion that sees no evil in racial injustice, prejudice, segregation, indifference to the poor, and unconcern about people's welfare.

If many evangelical Christians of today were true to their profession, like Martin Luther they might find it hard to accept the Book of James, thus posing a problem of authenticity of a portion of the Bible. After all, one of the real tests of our view of Scripture is whether we are willing to be obedient to its teaching. Aren't we inconsistent when we accept a book as truly inspired but fail to heed its precepts? James cuts deep into the core of ethical Christian living and has no patience with an accurate orthodoxy that has no ethical or social concern. or social concern.

The author of the Book of James was a robust, vital, energetic man. James, the brother of our Lord, is generally accepted to be the author. Paul said that the Lord Jesus appeared to James after His resurrection (I Cor. 15:7). He is mentioned in the Gospels (Matt. 13:55; John 5:7). He was among those who gathered in Jerusalem to wait for the promise of the Father (Acts 1:14). Paul conferred with him in Jerusalem three years after his own conversion (Gal. 1:19). Eventually James became a leader in the Jerusalem church, holding a position that commanded great power, if not the supreme authority. He presided over the Jerusalem conference concerned with admission of the Gentiles into the church (Acts 15:6-29), and listened to the missionary reports of Paul (Acts 21:18). He had a strongly Jewish outlook and knew the pulse of the earliest church.

It is easy to see therefore why James was so impatient with a faith that did not produce good works. He no doubt was present on the day of Pentecost, when the church experienced its first burst of life. He could recall that day when three thousand people were added to the church (Acts 2:41). He saw many profess Christ, among whom no doubt were many whose profession went no further than mental acceptance of what they heard. He wrote his letter to combat this heresy.

James wrote to a group of Christians who had over-reacted to the Jewish legalistic system. It could be that many, in the enthusiasm of their faith in Christ, had neglected simple obedience. James knew the dangers of false doctrine, but he also knew that an almost greater danger was to live with a heresy which deluded a person into believing that salvation was based on an intellectual acceptance that did not require active and outward obedience. Perhaps this is the rankest heresy of all—a heresy that still plagues the church of Jesus Christ. More than ever we need the message of James with its poignant, ethical, practical, and vibrant teaching!

1. Can You Pass the Test?

> *"Count it all joy, my brethren, when you meet various trials, for you know that the testing of your faith produces steadfastness. And let steadfastness have its full effect, that you may be perfect and complete, lacking in nothing. Blessed is the man who endures trial, for when he has stood the test he will receive the crown of life which God has promised to those who love him"* (James 1:2, 3, 4, 12).

To some people, for a person to be happy about his problems and difficulties is as crazy as stepping in front of a subway train. It is one thing to acknowledge pain, but to be happy about having it is incomprehensible. But why suffer pain? By using pain-killing pills and mind-dulling beverages we can push pain, whether physical or mental, into the background. Facing problems or pain is easily remedied with a few cocktails or a dose of drugs. Why face problems when science has created ways to forget them—or at least to help us ignore them?

For most people, trials, temptations, pain, and difficulties are experiences that must be avoided at all costs. Therefore modern man treats them as enemies to be battled and resisted by any means. The fastest and easiest way to escape from one's problems is to be tranquilized away from them. If that does not help, psychotherapy may help a person understand his problems by perhaps finding a cause in the recesses of his early childhood. Some of these methods are good, some are questionable, and some are outright ludicrous.

Using modern medical techniques to reduce pain and tension is certainly not wrong. Many people, however, have never faced themselves squarely but have instead resorted to drugs and forms of psychological repression. They relieve only the symptoms and don't get at the real cause of their problems. Science has provided an escapism that has kept people from facing difficulties realistically. At the same time scientists have accused religion of being merely an escapism for the fearful and superstitious. Yet science itself has provided a way of escape for many who have been relieved of pain (through pain-killing drugs) while still victims of the painful disease.

People try to avoid facing the real world. Men lose themselves in their business life in order to forget an unfortunate family problem. Women, left alone at home, become bored and get addicted to alcohol. Young people seek drugs to find deeper meaning in life. This emphasis on avoiding all pain and stress has made masses of people unable to cope with the real problems of life. When the drugs wear off and the money is no longer available for psychiatric treatment, many people blow their mind and are worse off than before.

When the apostle James said to "count it all joy" when you meet difficulties, he was telling Christians

11

they should face their problems realistically. They should treat problems head on as valid experiences sent from God for a purpose. James says that the Christian should look at such problems as "happy occasions," not as a time to retreat into self-doubt and defeat. A trial can be an opportunity—a time of joy rather than fear. This is an absolute about-face from the unbeliever's way of facing trial.

How can a person be happy when facing a trial or while in pain? Isn't this an unrealistic command? Is James trying to fool us? First of all, James is not a sadist. He did not say Christians should seek pain and trouble for themselves in order to gain some kind of pleasure. Few people want problems. No normal individual likes pain or persecution. Normal people try to avoid pain. There's no sin in looking for comfort and ease.

James is being honest and realistic. He says to Christians, "You are no better than anyone else. You are human beings. You are going to face trials like everyone else. You are not immune from the frailties of mankind. But, you have an advantage over others because you have a hope that they do not share. And this hope gives you a reason to be happy when you face various trials. Because you have Jesus Christ, you don't have to sink into a morbid melancholy or depression when troubles come." "Hence we can confidently say, 'The Lord is my helper, I will not be afraid; what can man do to me?' " (Heb. 13:6).

Men face three kinds of trial. There is (1) physical trial. This usually comes as bodily harm. While this kind of outward persecution is not as prevalent as in former times, it still exists in various places. Christians in China,

North Vietnam, North Korea, Cuba, and other nations under atheistic and fascist governments often experience this kind of trial.

There is (2) social trial. Christians in some communities have been looked upon as freaks and misfits. Some segments of society have written off Christianity as a superstitious relic left from the Dark Ages. Christians have been categorized as obscurantists and therefore left out socially by many of the world's so-called elite. All too often Christians themselves have helped perpetuate this attitude by holding a narrow view of "worldliness." Peter warned that if Christians suffer it should not be because they deserve to for their own wrong doing, but because they are taking a positive stand for Christ and His cross (I Peter 3:14-17).

Another form of trial is (3) psychological. Bodily pain is only one of Satan's tools to break down a Christian's faith. More often he uses pressures on the mind to demoralize a Christian's will. Mental torment can lead us into far more anguish than physical torture. The indifference of a loved one can bring more pain than many of the most bizarre tortures. Torture of the mind is perhaps more cruel and devastating than that done to the body, for it can be administered subtly. A mentally tortured person has greater difficulty finding relief—especially when he keeps his anguish inside himself.

Psychological warfare has been practiced in some form since the days of Genghis Khan. During World War I, all sides tried to influence the enemy by propaganda techniques. In World War II, G.I.'s listened to Tokyo Rose on the radio as she tried to demoralize United States troups. In the Korean War, the North Koreans developed brainwashing techniques to get American soldiers to desert their country. Christian people also at times are brainwashed by the world into thinking that life will be restricted by the teachings of Christianity.

James says that trials bring out endurance and steadfastness in us. "Faith worketh patience" (1:3 KJV). We may wonder why it is important for us to grow in patience. Why do we need to be patient? Life today is fast moving, hectic, and active; there is no time for waiting. Contemporary society is impatient about everything. People want things *now,* so they use credit cards until they get chin deep in debt. They make impatient demands to end such things as pollution, war, disease, and crime *now,* often without regard for all the consequences, ramifications, and obstacles.

Our impatience with all these sores of modern life perpetuates our problems. We fail to learn through circumstances. We don't take the time to think through problems. We demand cleaner lakes and ban the use of phosphates, only to pollute our water immediately with other substitutes. We speed up crop growth in order to feed the starving millions of the world, and by our overuse of chemical fertilizers we pollute our rivers, streams, and oceans. We are so impatient we don't let nature recycle itself. We speed up nature's way, but eventually we pay for our impatience—often too late.

Christians need patience and endurance to face the agonizing and crucial stresses of life. Why does God permit trials and suffering? Because He wants to prepare us for the unexpected, for the abuses and the tragedies we must face as humans. The "various trials" that come happen for our learning and instruction. They teach us discipline, trust, and patience so we can bear life at all its levels of intensity. In I Corinthians 10:13 we read, "God is faithful, and he will not let you be tempted beyond your strength, but with the temptation will also provide the way of escape, that you may be able to endure it."

A person who has not learned how to cope with trials soon becomes disillusioned with life and despairs of hope. He loses touch with God and may even doubt or deny God's existence or personal interest in man. He quickly accuses God of not caring, or of being weak. Failure to understand the purpose of trails has led many people to agnosticism and cynicism. Modern novels, drama, theater, and movies are full of themes that depict life as a senseless, meaningless trip that goes nowhere and produces nothing but despair.

Joy during trials is a rare quality and is not easy to find or develop. We have become so accustomed to affluence and security that we have failed to grasp the meaning of suffering. Through such failure we do a great disservice to others by sheltering them from the problems and perplexities of life. In contrast to this, the apostle Paul knew the value of trial. He said, "We rejoice in our sufferings, knowing that suffering produces endurance, and endurance produces character, and character produces hope, and hope does not disappoint us, because God's love has been poured into our hearts through the Holy Spirit which has been given to us" (Rom. 5:3-5).

Christians understand and teach that God controls all of life, even though God's purposes may not always be evident. Christians look upon life's trials as opportunities to try to understand the intricate mysteries of life. They know that the answers are not always evident, but they hope and trust in God who has promised to bring all things together. In Romans 8:28 Paul says, "We know that in everything God works for good with those who love him, who are called according to his purpose."

James encourages Christians to "let patience have her perfect work" (KJV). The Living Bible puts it this way, "So let it grow, and don't try to squirm out of your problems. For when your patience is finally in full bloom, then you will be ready for anything, strong in character, full and complete."

Patience during trials helps develop a strength of character that cannot come by education alone. The hard knocks of life have their purpose. Though they are painfully real, they are not always as bad as they appear while we are experiencing them. Our attitude toward the events that come into our lives molds our character and helps determine future actions. How we view trials and difficulties therefore has tremendous effect upon what we are becoming.

Children who have been sheltered by parents during their growing years are often severly handicapped when they are left to themselves as young adults. Maturity of character is something learned through many experiences. If we do not experience a certain amount of tension in our growing years we cannot build up strength to bear the ever larger problems that are inevitable in life.

A child needs to sense some pain to protect him from serious injury. The sudden sensation of a warming iron or stove, a scraped knee or a bruised elbow—all these may have practical value to teach a child about more serious dangers. In this sense suffering is good because it is instructive.

In much the same manner God uses hardships and suffering to instruct us and develop our character. He

16

does this because He loves us (Prov. 3:12). The writer to the Hebrews recognized this truth and admitted that God's "chastening" was not "joyous" but would lead to the "peaceable fruit of righteousness" (Heb. 12:11).

In the story of the prodigal son, the wayward youth was allowed to reach the depths of frustration before he came to see that his freedom and independence from family ties had led him to the bottom of life's potentialities. His high and loose living couldn't last forever. God brought him to the brink of disaster before He led him to the rewarding path of repentance and obedience. The prodigal's experience, though contrary to God's will, led to trial and frustration. But it was this very experience that initiated his return and growth as a respected and useful son.

It should not surprise us to find ourselves stymied by God. It is not His callousness, but His concern that allows us to experience bitter circumstances. Through them we learn the patience that perfects us. In them we learn how to face life realistically. We learn dependence not on ourselves alone, but on God who works in and through all things for our good and His glory.

LET'S DISCUSS

1. Define a trial. What is the difference between trials and temptations? What types of trials do Christians experience?
2. What are some trials you have experienced? What effect did they have upon you? Did your trials ever cause any bitterness against God?
3. How do trials benefit us as Christians? Why do you think God uses this method for training us? Do you think there is a better way?

17

4. Why do people often become bitter against God because of their misfortunes? Is this a misunderstanding or misconception about life? about God?

5. What preparation can we make to help us face trials and sorrows with a spirit of joy and contentment? Is this really possible? What are some examples?

6. Why does James place emphasis on trials as a means of teaching patience? Would we be more patient if difficulties didn't mess up our lives?

7. What is the relation of sin to suffering? Does evidence of suffering imply the presence of sin?

8. What changes in character are produced when a person experiences trials and suffering? Do most people respond in the same way? (Compare David and Saul.)

9. What comfort do we have from Scripture that assures us of God's purpose in our trials?

10. How do the trials and oppressions of certain minority groups, such as blacks, relate to trials as understood from a Christian point of view? Should they be looked upon as the same kind of trials that we experience as Christians? Why or why not?

2. So You're Tempted

*"Let no one say when he is tempted, 'I am
tempted by God'; for God cannot be tempted
with evil and he himself tempts no one; but
each person is tempted when he is lured and
enticed by his own desire. Then desire when it
has conceived gives birth to sin; and sin when it
is full-grown brings forth death.*

*"Do not be deceived, my beloved brethren.
Every good endowment and every perfect gift is
from above, coming down from the Father of
lights with whom there is no variation or shad-
ow due to change"* (James 1:13-17).

Popular comedian Flip Wilson comically voices a common viewpoint of wrongdoing. "The devil made me do
it," he says with an impish grin. Of course, blaming the
devil for personal wrongdoing isn't simply a comedian-
developed punch line. It was first mouthed in the Garden of Eden when Eve seriously declared, "The serpent
beguiled me, and I ate" (Gen. 3:13).

How far should we go in blaming the devil for our

19

sinning? Is he really responsible? What is his role in the lives of humans? Do we overemphasize his powers or make too little of them? Is he the master plotter behind every temptation—both major and minor?

Ever since that first fruit-eating experience by Eve, Satan has been in the business of tempting people to go against God's plans. He has sought to thwart what God has intended for man. Sometimes this tempting is to completely falsify the plan of God (see Gen. 3:3-5); at other times it is to fulfill a temporary want when an eternal need demands fulfillment (Matt. 4:3, 4).

Scripture constantly pictures the devil as the tempter. Possibly this role is most clearly stated in the encounter Jesus had with Satan in the wilderness. He is specifically called *the tempter* (Matt. 4:3). He spelled out what he wanted Christ to do and dangled pleasant rewards before Christ—in exchange for Christ's allegiance. Jesus clearly told him that it is written, "You shall not tempt the Lord your God" (Matt. 4:7).

Scripture speaks of people giving in to Satan. In Acts 5:3, Peter asks Ananias, "Why has Satan filled your heart to lie to the Holy Spirit?" John tells us that the devil put it in the heart of Judas to betray Christ (John 13:2). Paul informed Timothy that "some have already strayed after Satan" (I Tim. 5:15). John, in Revelation 12:9, describes Satan as "the deceiver of the whole world."

Paul tells the Ephesians to "give no opportunity to the devil" (Eph. 4:27), after warning them about controlling their anger. In the Christian armor text, Paul tells the Ephesian Christians to "put on the whole armor of God, that you may be able to stand against the wiles [clever acts and suggestions] of the devil" (Eph.

6:10-17). Giving the qualifications of a bishop, Paul says, "He must not be a recent convert, or he may be puffed up with conceit and fall into the condemnation of the devil . . . or he may fall into reproach and the snare of the devil" (I Tim. 3:6, 7). In II Timothy 2:26, Paul hopes that opponents of the Lord's servants "may escape from the snare of the devil, after being captured by him to do his will."

On the opposite end of the tug-of-war are the people who blame God for all their personal actions, whether good or evil. Since God made us as we are, they say, He is responsible for everything we think and do. They even say that since God created Satan, God is responsible for all evil. They fail to acknowledge the ingenuity of God's creative powers. If He created beings in His likeness, able to make good choices, He had to allow for the possibility of opposite or evil choices. Without this possibility, no person is truly free.

James unequivocally states that God had no part in causing man to sin. He says, "Let no one say when he is tempted, 'I am tempted by God'; for God cannot be tempted with evil and he himself tempts no one." To say that God tempts man is a contradiction, for He is perfect in Himself. God is untemptable and is incapable of any contact or contract with evil. Rather than bringing temptation, God works for man's good, according to James (1:17).

God is the giver of good gifts. He is the "Father of lights." Jesus proclaimed Himself as "the light of the world." He declared that those who follow Him will not walk in darkness but will possess the light of life (John 8:12). They will possess the power, through the indwelling Christ, to do good. Those who do not have that light

21

walk according to the powers of darkness—the powers of evil. Their source of spiritual energy is self or Satan, not God.

Let's face it, most of our temptations lie within ourselves. We often encourage temptation to germinate and blossom to its full fruit—sin. Though sin originated with Satan and was handed down from generation to generation, we have to take the full blame for how we react to it. We are not automatons; we have the power of choice and are responsible for all of our actions. It isn't as simple as Flip Wilson's "the devil made me do it" and it is never "the Lord caused me to yield."

James says, "Each person is tempted when he is lured and enticed by his own desire." This means we are tempted because we want to be. Our desires are evil. The temptations originate within. In fact, James makes no mention in his entire book that Satan is the source of temptation, even though he unquestionably was ortho-dox in his theology. He deprives sinners of any excuse for their sins. While it is true that Satan is indirectly involved in temptation, James stresses its exclusive in-ward nature. We are tempted because we delight in pleasing self and fulfilling our own sinful desires.

Jesus clearly stated that defilement is from within. "There is nothing outside a man which by going into him can defile him; but the things which come out of a man are what defile him. . . . Whatever goes into a man . . . enters, not his heart but his stomach. . . . For from within, out of the heart of man, come evil thoughts, fornication, theft, murder, adultery, coveting, wickedness, deceit, licentiousness, envy, slander, pride, foolishness. All these evil things come from within, and they defile a man" (Mark 7:15, 18, 19, 21, 22, 23).

22

Temptation is caused by desire. When desire is not controlled by God it is easily the basis for sinful action. A desire for some pleasure, for recognition, for power over others—any type of desire, if it is cultivated for self-centered gratification, will open you to temptation. Temptation originates within. When self-centered desire seeks gratification, an amazing number of possibilities open up for fulfillment. One can be creative to do evil as well as to do good.

We ought not boast that we are never tempted to commit gross sins. Pride is sin—so is self-deception. Paul warned us, "Let any one who thinks that he stands take heed lest he fall" (I Cor. 10:12). Perhaps our sins are mostly inward and don't immediately affect others as does adultery, theft, or murder. Nevertheless they are sins. We can be as guilty by yielding to the temptation to harbor these attitudes as actually committing outward, physically destroying acts. Inward enticing and luring is just as strong and sometimes more difficult to drop.

If we are honest we must blame ourselves when we fall into temptation. We must take the full responsibility for our own corrupt desires. It is precisely at this point that the Lord can help us most. That's when the truth of I Corinthians 10:13 can become vitally powerful in our experience: "No temptation has overtaken you that is not common to man. God is faithful, and he will not let you be tempted beyond your strength, but with the temptation will also provide the way of escape, that you may be able to endure it."

LET'S DISCUSS

1. Hebrews 4:15 says that "we have not a high priest who is unable to sympathize with our weaknesses,

but one who in every respect has been tempted as we are, yet without sinning." Explain how Jesus was tempted in every respect like us.

2. Since Jesus had a sinless nature while upon the earth, how can He understand the problems we have in resisting temptations?

3. Why can't God be tempted by evil? Why can't we blame Him for individual temptation?

4. What did Jesus mean in the prayer He taught His disciples, "Lead us not into temptation" (Matt. 6:13), and by the words in the garden, "Pray that you may not enter into temptation" (Matt. 26:41)?

5. If temptations originate within, how can we fortify ourselves against them? What kinds of inner changes do we need? Where does our faith in Christ fit in?

6. What place does the devil have in temptation in our lives? Can we blame him for any temptations? How? Which ones?

7. James 4:7 tells us that we are to resist the devil. Will this help in overcoming temptations? In what specific, practical ways can the Christian resist the devil? Is there ever a time when he'll flee so far that he won't bother the Christian? When?

8. Should we pray for victory over specific temptations? How should we pray? How can we tell when we have the victory?

9. How does James explain the progression in temptation from desire to death (1:14, 15)? Is this true experientially? Explain.

10. If the same temptation keeps cropping up in our experience, what does this indicate about our desires? Would temptations soon die if we eliminated the desires? Explain how this can be done.

11. Does physical and emotional health have anything to do with either the coming of temptations or the power to overcome them? Can we blame submission to temptation on some factors outside of inner desires? Would this remove moral responsibility?

12. What pattern can we develop to resist temptations? Must each one be resisted as it comes up? Can you give some examples how you resist or avoid temptation?

13. Is there ever a time when we'll be free from temptation? If so, when will that be? Can we attain sinless perfection in this life?

3. Genuine Religion

"But be doers of the word, and not hearers only, deceiving yourselves. For if any one is a hearer of the word and not a doer, he is like a man who observes his natural face in a mirror; for he observes himself and goes away and at once forgets what he was like. But he who looks into the perfect law, the law of liberty, and perseveres, being no hearer that forgets but a doer that acts, he shall be blessed in his doing.

"If any one thinks he is religious, and does not bridle his tongue but deceives his heart, this man's religion is vain. Religion that is pure and undefiled before God and the Father is this: to visit orphans and widows in their affliction, and to keep oneself unstained from the world" (James 1:22-27).

Several years ago New York University labeled its liberal arts division "The College of Arts and Pure Science." It called its engineering school "The College of Applied Science." Some educators disapproved of the two designations because they implied a gap between theory and practice.

A struggle constantly goes on between those who expound theories and those who believe practice to be more important—whether in the field of science, education, or religion. It's not difficult to find those who point accusing fingers at theorists for being impractical. Theorists are labeled eggheads. Contrariwise, theorists accuse practitioners of oversimplifying life.

Sometimes Christianity is criticized for being theoretical, for promising "pie in the sky." But other fields—such as the social sciences, history, and philosophy—have similar problems between practice and theory. In religion, one of the difficulties is the use of terms. We falsely assume that people understand such concepts as salvation, born again, regeneration, sanctification, and justification. Theological language can become a barrier to genuine faith, for in itself it cannot demonstrate what religion is all about.

Down-to-earth Christians, whose faith is active in the world, are often criticized by more conservative minded Christians for practicing a so-called social gospel. The practical Christians' concern for applying love leads the conservative critics to the idea that they are neglecting the theological basis of the Christian life. James bridges the gap between these two emphases and seeks to show that religion is neither based on a narrow believism nor a nebulous activism.

The Pharisees of Christ's day were basically conservative traditionalists. They adhered to the letter of Old Testament law. They looked with suspicion on anyone who deviated from their rigid rules. Jesus, who was a radical activist, was a threat to all they held dear. He accused the Pharisees of hypocrisy because they were theorists whose beliefs, even though pure in concept, lacked practical application. Their practices were out of harmony with their theories. They had highly developed theories about brotherly love and yet they hated love personified in Jesus Christ.

James, like Jesus, continually attacked religious theorists. He said that the hearer (and we can assume that this could easily include those who theorized on the gospel) deceived himself about the reality of his religious experience if he was not a doer of the Word. In chapter 2, James talks about dead faith that goes no further than pure theory.

James pictures the "hearer only" religionist as a man who looks into a mirror and then forgets what he saw reflected back at him. Normally, unless we have been brainwashed by TV advertising, a man soon forgets what he looks like after viewing himself in a mirror. He walks away and forgets himself, thinking he's quite presentable to the world.

The "hearer only" type see themselves in the mirror of God's perfect Word but do nothing about their condition. They come face to face with the Bible and what it says about their relationship to Jesus Christ, but they go away and do nothing about it.

To look into the mirror of the Bible involves an obligation. Bible reading is excellent and necessary for proper Christian development, but it cannot be an end in itself. The Bible always demands a human response. No man can come to the New Testament and remain neutral. He, of course, can reject it and reap the eternal consequences; but if he accepts its truths he also accepts the requirements to put his faith into action. A genuine Christian cannot come to the Bible, shrug his shoulders about changing his ways, and then walk away unconcerned.

Nor should we take a cursory glance into God's Word—like a quick look into a mirror before we rush off to catch the next commuter train in the morning. A concerned person—one whom the Lord uses to make an impact on the world—takes a long, thorough look into the mirror of the Word. He remembers what he saw—both his condition before God and his involvement in society—and then goes out to be a doer.

The true hearer of the Word "looks into the perfect law, the law of liberty, and perseveres," This perfect law sets such a man free from sin and selfishness. The commands of Christ are a "law of liberty" because he has been set free to serve. He accepts this law without compulsion and is eager to obey it because of his love toward God. He listens to what God says to him and doesn't forget the command of God. He becomes a "doer that acts" and is happy in the doing. A doer of the Word is an activist in his faith, and his "genuine religion" works itself out in society. The following quote sums up the role of the doer of the Word in society:

"Being a Christian is more than believing doctrines and following rules. It is based upon a vital relationship with Jesus Christ that motivates a person to proper involvement both with God and with men. . . .

"God desires us to love and worship Him, but we cannot do this apart from true love and active concern for people. The Bible plainly tells us that love for God motivates a love for men. If we are without love and compassion for men, God's love does not abide in us (I John 3:17). To ignore social concern is to deny our

29

faith. Concern for others is intertwined throughout the fabric of the Bible. . . .

". . . action must follow talk. It is not enough to propose that we have the right answers. We must back up beliefs with deeds. We are to be doers of the Word. . . .

"We should take an active part in community programs on sex education and environmental pollution. We must cooperate with local officials to reduce crime and drug addiction. We must encourage local churches to cooperate with others in welfare and aid programs. We must be willing to speak out on touchy and unpopular issues. . . . Concern for others is the natural outgrowth of Christian experience and expression."[1]

James describes genuine religion: "Religion that is pure and undefiled before God and the Father is this: to visit orphans and widows in their affliction." He does not describe genuine religion from the perspective of worship, though one can be sure that his perspective was vertically as well as horizontally inspired. Surely, as a leader in the early church, James accepted true religion to include outward worship as an expression of the faith that is in the heart, but he went further. He included such things as controlling one's speech and practical service to others as part of being religious.

James was acquainted with the psalmist's words: "Father of the fatherless and protector of widows is God in his holy habitation. God gives the desolate a home to dwell in; he leads out the prisoners to prosperity" (Ps. 68:5, 6). He knew God as one concerned about those in

---

[1] Krutza, William J., and Di Cicco, Philip P. *Facing the Issues 3*. Grand Rapids: Baker Book House, 1970, pp. 3, 4.

need. His Jesus came to heal the sick, preach the gospel to the poor, proclaim release to the captives, recover sight to the blind, set at liberty those who are oppressed (Luke 4:18). Possibly he heard Jesus say, "Come, O blessed of my Father, inherit the kingdom prepared for you from the foundation of the world; for I was hungry and you gave me food, I was thirsty and you gave me drink, I was a stranger and you welcomed me, I was naked and you clothed me, I was sick and you visited me, I was in prison and you came to me" (Matt. 25:34-36).

James did not put orphans and widows in a special category, saying, "Now, if you help these, you'll be religious." Orphans and widows were simply two good examples of destitute people who needed special attention and help. They were the most deprived, the most vulnerable to exploitation. They could not return kindness for kindness. They had little or no social status. They were a drag on society and the church.

James describes pure religion in terms of helping the helpless. This was following in the footsteps of Jesus Christ more than anything else. Jesus paid attention to the helpless, whether a woman taken in adultery or one with a incurable blood disease, lepers, cripples, or blind beggars. Pure religion is being like Jesus Christ.

James teaches that compassionate service to the needy in the community demonstrates the clearest manifestation of pure religion. Compassion is always linked to the love of God toward men. Jesus constantly "looked with compassion" on needy people. Following in the pattern of the Savior in this way, we give real evidence that we have taken His philosophy of life; that we have been transformed by His life-giving power.

31

When the scribes asked Christ what commandment is the first of all, He answered, "The first is, 'Hear, O Israel: The Lord our God, the Lord is one; and you shall love the Lord your God with all your heart, and with all your soul, and with all your mind, and with all your strength.' The second is this, 'You shall love your neighbor as yourself.' There is no other commandment greater than these" (Mark 12:29-31).

The Good Samaritan story clearly indicates that our neighbors are those who are the most needy around us. To love our neighbor as we love ourselves means caring for and sharing in his needs. Jesus declared with His lips and life that it is impossible to love God and at the same time be hard-hearted toward those in desperate need. To meet the needs of the destitute is one way to demonstrate that "the love of God is shed abroad in our hearts." Words and deeds go hand in hand. Both issue from the heart and reveal our genuine religion.

It is this kind of religion that, paradoxically, while getting its hands dirty through ministering to the destitute, also keeps "oneself unstained from the world." Having a Christ-like attitude toward the needy is the best way to develop a spiritual insulation from the world's every-man-for-himself philosophy. This keeps a person's perspective straight—looking upward through an activist faith and looking outward toward needy people in the application of that faith. With such a stance, one won't become contaminated by the philosophy of the world. Genuine religion is activistic as it relates to both God and needy men. That kind of religion gets an A rating from the apostle James.

LET'S DISCUSS

1. How much emphasis should we place on the theoretical knowledge of Christianity? Should we concentrate more on being doers than being believers? Would this change our present approaches in Sunday school and other church organizations?
2. To what extent can we say that service to others purifies one's faith? How much service is needed to qualify for James's concept of "pure religion"?
3. Does a "hearer only" have salvation? If not, does salvation depend on being a doer? Does this take anything away from the concept of salvation being a free gift of God?
4. What kind of "doing" is James suggesting? What kind of "doing" does Scripture suggest the Christian should practice?
5. Why is it so much more difficult to practice our faith than to expound it and even witness about it?
6. Is social welfare a responsibility of the church today? How much? Should we leave welfare work and expenses and programs to the government?
7. What types of programs should a local church maintain to take care of its needy on a continuing basis? Are present programs adequate to meet the needs in your community?
8. Does James mean that service has to be limited to helping destitute people? What is "service" in the broad sense of the term?
9. From the viewpoint of fulfilling James's concept of "pure religion," does our activity have to be done through a church related ministry? Should we con-

sider purely social service as being apart from church obligations?

10. Why is service to others not a criterion for membership in a local church? Should it be? Why or why not?

4. Watch out for Partiality

"My brethren, show no partiality as you hold the faith of our Lord Jesus Christ, the Lord of glory. For if a man with gold rings and in fine clothing comes into your assembly, and a poor man in shabby clothing also comes in, and you pay attention to the one who wears the fine clothing and say, 'Have a seat here, please,' while you say to the poor man, 'Stand there,' or, 'Sit at my feet,' have you not made distinctions among yourselves, and become judges with evil thoughts? Listen, my beloved brethren. Has not God chosen those who are poor in the world to be rich in faith and heirs of the kingdom which he has promised to those who love him? But you have dishonored the poor man. Is it not the rich who oppress you, is it not they who drag you into court? Is it not they who blaspheme that honorable name by which you are called?

"If you really fulfil the royal law, according to the scripture, 'You shall love your neighbor

as yourself,' you do well. But if you show partiality, you commit sin, and are convicted by the law as transgressors. For whoever keeps the whole law but fails in one point has become guilty of all of it. For he who said, 'Do not commit adultery,' said also, 'Do not kill.' If you do not commit adultery but do kill, you have become a transgressor of the law. So speak and so act as those who are to be judged under the law of liberty. For judgment is without mercy to one who has shown no mercy; yet mercy triumphs over judgment" (James 2:1-13).

One of the basic teachings of the Bible is that all men are equal before God. No accident of nature, no stricture of society, no judgment of individual men can alter the truth that God respects all men equally as objects of His care and love. Christians should be the first to recognize this truth and to put it into practice. Sadly, however, Christians often seem to be the last ones to consider its implications and to translate it into practical action. If Christians would practice impartiality they would go far toward eliminating many injustices of our society.

James illustrates the hypocrisy of partiality. He says that we should not have "respect of persons." Modern translations use different terms, such as "show no partiality," "have no favoritism," "make no distinctions," "show no snobbery" (2:1).

When a group of Christians have a meeting, says James, and a finely dressed, obviously wealthy man of eminent stature appears, and at the same time another man shabbily dressed and lowly in rank also appears, and you give preference to the rich man over the poor one, you are making an unwarranted distinction. Since James wrote to Christians who were still meeting together in local synagogues, he uses the word "assembly" (literally, "synagogue") to refer to their meeting for instruction, fellowship, and worship.

Jesus implied several times during His ministry that making distinctions between rich and poor, between lofty leaders and common people was popular among the Jews. His reference to the ostentatious giving by the pharisaical rich compared to the honest, heartfelt giving by the poor widow, and His word about the practice of long prayers spoken primarily for men's ears in contrast to the simple, realistic prayer of the sinful tax-gatherer are cases in point.

Are we any less guilty today when we make distinctions between people, both within and without the church? It is not just between rich and poor; there is also the strong prejudice of race—especially between blacks and whites. Many Christians have yet to accept the biblical teaching on the question of race. While a certain amount of lip service is paid to equality, many white Christians still believe themselves to be superior to black people. Blacks are still unwelcome in many churches. White congregations keep moving from interracial neighborhoods. White Christians move out of their urban communities into more pleasant suburban areas, leaving the inner city in a spiritual vacuum.

In our day of enlightened awareness about people, it seems a horrendous sin to look on others as inferior—especially when this is done by Christians who twist the Bible to support their prejudice. Nothing makes Christianity look so sick to the outside world as to have bigoted Christians defend race separation with Scripture texts. We would hope that this emphasis is disappearing from Christians who sincerely honor the Bible as God's revelation.

James points out that the poor, as a class, have been those most responsive to God (2:5). Throughout history it generally has been the poor who have been open to God's revelation. Jesus identified with the poor and was born of poor parents Himself. His relatives—Zechariah, Elizabeth, and John the Baptist—were all poor people. They were not recognized by the world for they were poor. Jesus grew up poor and remained economically poor until His death.

A recent article in *Psychology Today* on "God and the Poor" referred to the phenomenon of faith among the poor. The writer pointed out that in spite of the hardship and poverty that continually engulfed the poor, they still retained their faith in God. Widespread unbelief and atheism could be expected among the poor. On the contrary, as a group, they tend to exhibit more dependence on and faith in God than those who have greater material wealth. James refers to the poor as those who are "rich in faith" (2:5). Paul, referring to the Lord Jesus, said that "he became poor" that we "might become rich" (II Cor. 8:9). The poor referred to in the Bible were poor in material possessions but rich in spirit and faith.

Christianity is associated with the poor, not because there is virtue in material poverty, but because the poor are usually more receptive to God's message. The poor, by their very circumstances, cannot depend on their physical and material needs being fully supplied by their own efforts. Therefore they depend on the Lord more fully.

The rich and many middle-class people look down on the poor. They sit in their comfortable homes and criticize the poor for being what and where they are. It is easy to say glibly, "If the poor were more willing to work, they wouldn't be in such situations." This is a self-deluding attitude that insulates us from the truth and keeps us from seeing our responsibility to the poor. We forget that we may have depended on others to get us through difficult times. Poverty is no respecter of persons. Recently, employees within certain industries have felt the anguish of suddenly being without jobs even though they had a good education and many years of service with their companies.

Christians, because they have sought to uplift the poor, have historically been oppressed by rich rulers. This should motivate a sense of compassion for the poor. James says, "Is it not the rich who oppress you, is it not *they* who drag you into court?" If you want to verify that statement today, examine court records. See how few suits for damages (mental hardship, etc.) are brought by the poor. By far it is the well-to-do who can afford lawyers to bring suit against others (or against insurance companies) for relatively minor matters.

The poor, on the other hand, often go without proper remuneration. Because poverty limits education, the poor are not as worldly-wise as their richer counterparts. Consequently, as a group, they are willing to live and let live and not add burdens to others; for they know what it is to carry a heavy load.

James says, "Is it not they who blaspheme that honorable name by which you are called?" (2:7). To honor the rich by giving them preference over the poor is inconsistent with reality. It is the poor who have little or nothing, who should be honored and given the better places. It is the poor who should be given the breaks and the benefit of the doubt. If we are taking special actions to impress the rich among us, and neglecting the poor, we have a tremendous need to redirect our priorities more in line with James's sentiments.

The apostle James talked about fulfilling the "royal law," which was the Old Testament command stressed by Jesus, "You shall love your neighbor as yourself" (2:8). James, in essence, is holding up Scripture as our norm and standard in our relationships with others. The principle of loving one's neighbor and affirming others as better than ourselves (Phil. 2:3) extends throughout Scripture. The Jewish attitude toward Samaritans was a glaring breach of this commandment, one that Jesus attacked in His story of the Good Samaritan (Luke 10:30-37) and by His example with the woman at the well (John 4).

Showing partiality and prejudice through discrimination against the poor makes us guilty before God as much as breaking any one of the commandments. James stresses an important principle. Even though we do not organize our lives around the law of Moses, we do believe that the Ten Commandments are in force as God's eternal principles of morality for all men. Jesus showed that breaking the law is more than mere external transgression. Looking lustfully upon a woman is committing adultery (Matt. 5:28). According to John, hatred toward another human being is the same as murder (I John 3:15).

So partiality falls short of God's standard and breaks God's law of love. Giving the most beautiful praises to God will not ring true if we have hatred or discrimination in our hearts toward other human beings (I Cor. 13:1-3). It is completely incompatible for Christians to extol God's Word while denying the poor (like those in urban ghettos or depressed farm communities) the opportunity to worship with them. This is so contrary to James's teaching that it is strange how Christians who do this can say they believe the Bible as their rule of faith and practice.

The rich young ruler came to Jesus saying that he had kept all the commandments from his youth (Matt. 10:20), yet Jesus told him that he lacked "one thing." This involved a compassion for people. Jesus demanded that he be generous with the possessions God had given him (Matt. 10:21). "Keeping the faith" is not in itself rewarding in God's sight, unless one is able to keep every commandment (James 2:10). God's command is to "love our neighbor," whether rich or poor.

Our actions ought to match our words (2:12). We should practice what we preach in the light of God's standard of judgment. We cannot find mercy if we have not been merciful ourselves. "Judgment is without mercy to one who has shown no mercy" (v. 13). James gets at basic honesty in Christian living. If we say we are Christians, then we ought to demonstrate the basic principles of Christianity, especially in relation to those who are less fortunate than ourselves.

If we think more highly of ourselves than we ought to think (Rom. 12:4) and put down other people, we stand in judgment before God. If we see ourselves as God sees us, we will not put ourselves on pedestals. By the grace of God, we can see rightly what we are. We are what we are by the grace of God (I Cor. 15:10). But more than that, we will be able to see others in the light of God's compassionate love and care. We will see all men as objects of great worth and value, and therefore men who deserve equal treatment. We will not cater to those more heavily endowed with wealth and power because of their status in life. We will consider them only because they also are human beings whose spiritual needs should not be overlooked.

LET'S DISCUSS

1. Why do we find discrimination and partiality among Christians? Discuss some examples you have experienced or observed.
2. What practices within the church today tend to perpetuate inequality and discrimination between people?
3. How can we tell when our attitudes toward others are based on prejudices rather than fact? Why do we have more prejudice toward those who are poor?
4. What did James mean when he said that God chose the poor of this world to be "rich in faith and heirs of the kingdom" (2:5)? What bearing does this have on showing honor to the rich?
5. Is James's argument against the rich (2:6) valid today? In what ways? Discuss some examples.
6. What situations in the life of Christ show that He sought to break down artificial barriers between people?
7. Distinguish between and discuss cultural patterns of partiality adopted by Christians in contrast to customs actually taught in the Bible (e.g., segregation, social status).
8. Discuss James's concept of breaking "one point of

the law" as an act of guilt equal to transgressing the whole. How does this relate to the sin of partiality (cf. 2:9, 10)?

9. What is God's standard for us in relation to others (rich or poor, black or white) (James 2:8)? Is this realistic in the light of the various cultural outlooks in our day?

10. What can your church do to avoid acts of discrimination and partiality? Does your church or group have some such guarantee written into its constitution or bylaws? How can such guarantees be enforced?

5. Does Your Faith Work?

"What does it profit, my brethren, if a man says he has faith but has not works? Can his faith save him? If a brother or sister is ill-clad and in lack of daily food, and one of you says to them, 'Go in peace, be warmed and filled,' without giving them the things needed for the body, what does it profit? So faith by itself, if it has no works, is dead.

"But some one will say, 'You have faith and I have works.' Show me your faith apart from your works, and I by my works will show you my faith. You believe that God is one; you do well. Even the demons believe—and shudder. Do you want to be shown, you foolish fellow, that faith apart from works is barren? Was not Abraham our father justified by works, when he offered his son Isaac upon the altar? You see that faith was active along with his works, and faith was completed by works, and the scripture was fulfilled which says, 'Abraham believed God, and it was reckoned to him as

righteousness'; and he was called the friend of God. You see that a man is justified by works and not by faith alone. And in the same way was not also Rahab the harlot justified by works when she received the messengers and sent them out another way? For as the body apart from the spirit is dead, so faith apart from works is dead" (James 2:14-26).

For centuries theologians have argued whether a person is saved by faith or by good works. Much of the conflict over this question arises because of this text in the Letter of James. James seems to contradict the teaching of the apostle Paul, who clearly taught that a man was justified by faith apart from the deeds of the law (Rom. 5:1). Paul taught that man was "justified by his grace as a gift, through the redemption which is in Christ Jesus" (Rom. 3:24). This excluded any boasting, because works did not have anything to do with individual salvation. Salvation was based "on the principle of faith. For we hold that a man is justified by faith apart from . . . works of law" (Rom. 3:27, 28).

Paul's major arguments in the Letters to the Romans and the Galatians centered in combating the legalistic requirements certain Jews wanted to force upon Christianity. These legalists (Judaizers) wanted to make Jewish rituals mandatory for Christians. Paul taught that through Jesus' death on the cross, men were no longer bound to the ceremonial law of Moses, and that salvation was through His grace on the basis of faith (Eph. 2:8, 9; Titus 3:5; Gal. 3:10-29).

To those who emphasize Paul's teaching of justification by faith, James is most disturbing. In fact, they view James's teaching as contradictory to that of the apostle Paul. Martin Luther, the great Protestant reformer, rejected the Book of James. He had lived much of his life enslaved to a legalistic system that based salvation on meritorious good works. When he discovered Paul's teaching of justification by faith apart from works, it was such a dynamic and liberating experience that he could not accept any teaching which seemed to contradict his experience. He could not comprehend how James's emphasis on works could complement Paul's emphasis on faith and grace.

From our perspective, Martin Luther erred in rejecting the Book of James. Since his day, theologians and Bible scholars have concluded that James did not contradict Paul, but rather complemented him. The real key to understanding the difference between James and Paul rests in seeing the purpose of each author and distinguishing and defining how they used their terms.

When the apostle Paul speaks of faith he is referring to man's acceptance of God's action toward us in Christ. Faith is complete and open acceptance of what God has done, and is not based on anything we do. James is not criticizing this kind of faith. When he speaks of faith, it is primarily a reference to intellectual head-faith. He is not referring to faith as trust so much as faith as acceptance of factual truth. Faith, for James, was primarily in the intellect rather than the will—mental assent rather than committed trust.

When Paul speaks of works he usually refers to the "works of the law," the ceremonial rituals of Judaism. Paul, just as Jesus, battled against those who emphasized ritual cleanliness, sabbath regulations, and minute religious observance above obedience to the Word of God.

All these things Paul lumped into the category of the "works of the law." Paul, however, did speak of "good works" (Eph. 2:10), and in this sense he used "works" in the same manner as James. Works, for James, meant acts of love and mercy toward others.

The differences between James and Paul are largely attributable to the interpretation of these terms. Both men are basically saying the same thing, but with different emphases. Paul emphasizes *faith as that which produces good works* in a person who is justified. James emphasizes *good works as proof that a man has faith that justifies.*

The problem can be clarified a little further if we understand that the two men were opposing two different errors. Paul was opposing the strict legalistic requirements of the Judaizing element within Christianity. Therefore, he put strong emphasis on the grace of God and on our entrance into God's redemptive fellowship through faith in Christ's work on the cross. James, on the other hand, was speaking against the opposite perversion of the Christian faith known as antinomianism—antilaw. Incidentally, Paul also faced this problem. "Are we to continue in sin that grace may abound?" he asked in Romans 6:1. This heretical teaching proclaimed, "I have faith; therefore I don't have to worry about what I do." So James puts strong emphasis on the importance of *works as proving*—or in his terminology, "justifying"—a person's faith in Jesus Christ.

The question of the seeming contradiction between Paul and James has for the most part been answered satisfactorily by Bible scholars. The real problem for Christians today is whether we can resolve the outward contradiction of having a faith that is correct doctrinally, but weak or nonexistent when it comes to practical application and action. Often we miss James's argument completely by dwelling too long on the theological question. The overall emphasis of James is that *faith does not exist apart from works*. Faith and works must go together. Faith without works is ineffective—dead; and conversely, works without faith is a delusion. Faith and works must be considered together, not as separate entities.

The major truth that hits us when we study James's Letter is that faith is not genuine unless it is completed by positive action for good. James asserts that faith without good works is totally unprofitable. That kind of faith does not save (James 2:14). The King James Version is misleading when it puts James's question as "Can faith save him?" The Revised Standard Version hits the mark by translating it, "Can his faith save him?" James is not referring to a genuine kind of faith, for a faith apart from works is not true faith at all. He rightfully concludes that faith by itself, without works, is dead.

James illustrates his point saying that if there is a brother or sister who comes to you unclothed and without food, and you simply say to him, "Go in peace, be warmed and filled," and don't give him what he needs for his body—you are demonstrating that you do not have a vital faith. This illustration applies to many Christians today. In the name of doctrinally pure faith, many have been content to tell people about God's good news—by "giving them the gospel"—without thinking of putting any clothes on their backs or food in their mouths. Evangelism without social concern for the individual is proclaiming a dead religion, not biblical Christianity.

James's principle, however, applies not only to individuals but to the whole church as well. It is important that, as a body, the church show its faith not only by creeds and dogmas but also by outgoing and loving service to mankind.

James anticipates a person who might object, "You have faith and I have works" (2:18). He answers by posing a dilemma, "Show me your faith apart from your works." With this he silenced such objections, for how can one "show his faith" if faith is a relationship between God and man that is unseen? It is meaningless to talk about showing faith apart from tangible and observable action. So James, perhaps facetiously, says, "I by my works will show you my faith." This is not difficult to grasp because works can be examined and tested. Works show that faith exists, but faith apart from actions has no way of being proved. Talking about an experience of faith is not an adequate proof of the existence of faith.

Perhaps it would be good to make a distinction between *faith alone,* the concept emphasized by Luther, and *faith that is alone.* James refers to faith that is alone, not to the faith alone concept as taught by the reformers. Justification by faith alone refers to the act of justification by God on the basis of one's faith apart from the works of the law. This faith is not dependent on man's action but on God's. This kind of faith produces righteousness in the individual. On the other hand, faith that is alone is empty faith. It is mere head knowledge. Intellectual acceptance is the type of faith demons have, James points out. Even demons believe certain facts about God, which make them shudder; but this belief has no transforming qualities. Demon faith is empty faith, faith that merely acknowledges the existence of objective truth but places no value on it and refuses to commit one's life to it.

James cites two Old Testament characters to strengthen his position: Abraham (whom Paul referred to, to emphasize his doctrine of justification by faith) and Rehab the harlot. Paul quoted Genesis 15:6, "And he believed the Lord; and he reckoned it to him as righteousness," to show that righteousness was imputed to Abraham even before the law and circumcision were in effect. So the "works of the law" did not save Abraham (Rom. 4:2). It was his faith.

James uses Abraham to prove what at first might seem the very opposite. In fact James quotes the same verse the apostle Paul quotes (Gen. 15:6). But James wants to show that Abraham's act of offering his son Isaac was not separate from his faith. He says, "You see that faith was *active along with* his works, and faith was completed by works" (James 2:22). Could we describe Abraham's action apart from his faith in God's promise (Heb. 11:17, 18)? We are therefore forced to conclude that faith and works operate together. Putting one above the other distorts the true sense of New Testament teaching.

Using Rahab as an example of faith (Heb. 11:31) and good works seems strange, since little is made of her in the Old Testament. Yet the point James makes becomes clear. How could you prove that a harlot had faith, apart from some indication that she showed confidence in the messengers who visited her? Her protection of the spies was proof that she believed whatever message they conveyed to her. If she would have said, "Well, boys, you're very nice; but, you know, I got a business here and I really can't be troubled by some alien group of people . . . ," we could hardly attribute faith or good works to her. The fact that she acted favorably proved that she believed.

What will verify our faith? God says that we will all be judged according to *what we have done* (II Cor. 5:10); our works will be tested (I Cor. 3:12-15). God's judgment of Christians will be determined not by whether they have faith, but whether they have been faithful (Matt. 25:21).

Each man must ask himself, Upon what do I base my salvation? *Upon my own works?* That does not pass the test of God's imputed righteousness, for one slip against the law renders a person as guilty as if he had broken the whole (James 2:10). *Upon my own faith?* That too fails, for it does not pass the test of obedience and action. Real faith always produces works (fruit). Only a faith that is a committed trust in God's gracious provision in Jesus Christ as Savior, and which leads to obedience to God's will as demonstrated in loving acts toward other people, can be considered saving faith.

LET'S DISCUSS

1. What problems are raised between James's teaching and Paul's teaching in Romans on justification by faith? Do you think James was aware of Paul's writings? Would it have made any difference?
2. Can these two approaches be harmonized? Why or why not?
3. What was James's primary emphasis? Why do you think he stated his case with such strong language?
4. What are good works in the sense that James speaks

of them? How does this differ from Paul's use of the phrase "works of the law"?

5. Why could James and Paul both use Abraham to prove a different point of view? Were they contradictory?

6. What modern application can be made of the illustration in James 2:15, 16? Does this apply to the corporate church as well as to individuals? Does it apply to welfare programs? Why or why not?

7. How would you compare James's teaching that faith needs works for completion (2:17, 22) with the Protestant reformers' teaching of salvation by faith alone?

8. In the light of James's teaching on faith and good works, how can a person know that he is really saved? How can we avoid teaching salvation by works if we accept James's teaching?

9. How does Paul's teaching in I Corinthians 13:2, 3 apply to James's teaching on faith and works?

10. Discuss the ways Christians prove their faith. How much emphasis should we put on James's idea of proving our faith by our works? Does this emphasis have some dangers? Explain.

6. Having Difficulties with Your Tongue?

"Know this, my beloved brethren. Let every man be quick to hear, slow to speak, slow to anger, for the anger of man does not work the righteousness of God. Therefore put away all filthiness and rank growth of wickedness and receive with meekness the implanted word, which is able to save your souls. . . .

"Let not many of you become teachers, my brethren, for you know that we who teach shall be judged with greater strictness. For we all make many mistakes, and if any one makes no mistakes in what he says he is a perfect man, able to bridle the whole body also. If we put bits into the mouths of horses that they may obey us, we guide their whole bodies. Look at the ships also; though they are so great and are driven by strong winds, they are guided by a very small rudder wherever the will of the pilot directs. So the tongue is a little member and boasts of great things. How great a forest is set ablaze by a small fire!

"And the tongue is a fire. The tongue is an unrighteous world among our members, staining the whole body, setting on fire the cycle of nature, and set on fire by hell. For every kind of beast and bird, of reptile and sea creature, can be tamed and has been tamed by humankind, but no human being can tame the tongue—a restless evil, full of deadly poison. With it we bless the Lord and Father, and with it we curse men, who are made in the likeness of God. From the same mouth come blessing and cursing. My brethren, this ought not to be so. Does a spring pour forth from the same opening fresh water and brackish? Can a fig tree, my brethren, yield olives, or a grapevine figs?" (James 1:19-21; 3:1-12).

An old German proverb states, "There's many a slip 'twix cup and lip." One story attributes the saying to the practice of cutting an enemy's throat while he leaned back guzzling his stein of beer. The cup shielded his eyes, allowing the enemy to take advantage of his carelessness. Another familiar quip is, "Putting your foot in your mouth," referring to saying something that causes embarrassment either to you or to someone else. The use of words may have deep significance and dire consequences.

"Freudian slips" (innocent slips of the tongue) are usually laughed off, but perhaps they often have meaning far beyond the surface. Words tell us a lot about a person. We can tell how well informed a person is by his use of words; we can often tell where he comes from; we can tell if he is angry or happy; we can tell if he is logical or irrational. Through words we can discern character, style, motivations, emotions, desires, hatreds, loves, ambitions, and hopes.

Words are symbols of human personality. We cannot dismiss them as unimportant. To do so would deny the essence of our thought processes and unnecessarily separate a man's personality from his expression of it. Psychologists have used "word association" and "sentence completion" tests to delve into human personality. These tests have been successful in revealing problems and conflicts, and in assessing vocational interests and capabilities.

Jesus stressed the importance of words through this sobering statement: "By your words you will be justified, and by your words you will be condemned" (Matt. 12:37). In the light of this, it would be difficult to deny that there is no significance to idle chatter. Words are not only vehicles of thought, but the bearers of deep-seated feelings and motives. Words reveal what and who we are. How important therefore that we examine ourselves in the light of our words.

James begins his case about the importance of spoken words with an emphasis on the awesome responsibility of being in a position of authority and mastery over others. He says, "Let not many of you become teachers . . . for you know that we who teach shall be judged with greater strictness" (3:1). This gives some indication of the power of words. A teacher has an awesome responsibility for what he says, because of the effect of his words upon those who hear.

James's negative reasoning about becoming teachers sounds a bit reactionary at first. Isn't James contradicting the emphasis of Jesus and the New Testament? Jesus said that His disciples were to go into all nations and *teach* the good news. Paul encouraged teaching as a principle of church growth (II Tim. 2:2). James seems to be putting a damper on this New Testament emphasis.

We recognize that there is a constant need for teachers; but if we take this verse literally, how can we expect to encourage people to become Sunday school teachers or workers for other church ministries? Isn't James's philosophy a detriment to teacher recruitment? The answer is yes and no. Yes, in the sense that James warns against getting into a teaching position without understanding the responsibility demanded in presenting words and concepts that will affect the attitudes and behavior of others. To treat truth lightly, whether by design or ignorance, is a foolish error. A person who stands in a place of responsibility must have a sense of seriousness about his position. Irreparable damage to human souls may result from his words. A flippant person therefore should not be encouraged to enter so vital a ministry as teaching.

On the other hand, James's philosophy need not deter the person who understands the basic role of leadership and teaching. A leader understands himself. He is aware that "we all make many mistakes, and if any one makes no mistakes in what he says he is a perfect man" (3:2). Once he has leveled with himself as a person, he knows that he is dealing with others as persons who have tremendous worth to God. A man of tested character will face the challenge of teaching, though the risks of "greater" punishment (3:1) are ever present for him. In the long run, a few conscientious teachers will accomplish more for the kingdom of God

56

than thousands with good intentions, but little moral stamina, courage, and good sense.

Teachers have an influence that is difficult to overestimate, for they mold and guide people's minds. A few words can ignite a chain reaction of ideas and conclusions that can determine a person's course of action throughout his life. It does not take long to plant seeds of doubt in a human soul. James speaks of a small rudder turning a whole ship, and a small fire starting huge forests aflame (3:4, 5). So the human tongue, though small, can create great havoc.

A few enticing words from the serpent in the Garden of Eden plunged the human race into sin. A few words confirmed God's redemption complete on the cross when Jesus cried, "It is finished." A few words—"He is risen"—announced God's victory over death. Augustine was inspired to search Scripture when he heard a child's voice repeat the words, "Take up and read." Luther began a reformation of religion by obeying a few words from the Old Testament, quoted by the apostle Paul, "The just shall live by faith." Every day words determine the destiny of men: "guilty, not guilty"; "you're hired, you're fired"; "you win, you lose"; "come in, you're not allowed"; "I will, I won't." How important to remember the power of words!

James calls the tongue a "fire" (3:6) which, among all the parts of the body, is "unrighteous." One commentator states of verse 6, "All the sins in the world are ones in which speech plays a part, the unrighteous world being, as it were, focused in the tongue." The tongue, according to James, "sets on fire the cycle of nature." Perhaps a better paraphrase would be: it "upsets the natural balance of the natural sphere." In other words,

57

the tongue can make life miserable. And no doubt, for it is "set on fire by hell." How can you attribute anything worse to the tongue than to make hell its empowering source?

Humans love to tame things. We have domesticated animals. We have taught wild beasts to do astounding things. Animals have been taught to work for us as beasts of burden and to play for us as pets of pleasure. We are proud of these achievements; yet in contrast, no human being has been able to tame the tongue. No matter how cultivated and cultured the brain, the tongue still remains a "restless evil, full of deadly poison" (3:8).

Of course, we know that we can't tame the tongue as we tame animals. The tongue is controlled by man's mind. Animals respond to instinct and certain stimuli. The tongue cannot be so restricted because man's mind possesses a freedom that animals don't possess. Animals are not rational and do not exercise the power of choice. Men make choices—often the wrong ones—and sometimes speak before they think.

Not only is the tongue impossible to tame, but it can express the most fickle thoughts of the human mind. The tongue can bless and curse in the same breath (3:10). Because this trait of engaging in inconsistent speech appears in many church members, untold numbers of people have been hardened against Christ. Nothing can ruin a person's testimony quicker than to be hypocritical in his speech. A common complaint against the church is that it is "made up of hypocrites." While that accusation is hardly applicable to the whole church, there are enough people in the church whose deeds don't match their words to give a bad name to the whole church.

Children are quick to detect inconsistencies in parental speech. How often they hear their parents pray, sing, and praise God in church services, but within an hour after getting home they hear gossip, angry words, and even cursing. Because of such inconsistencies at home, some young people have lost faith in the church. They have not seen enough evidence in their parents' speech to prove that parents mean what they say. Whenever we lose our temper or remain angry over long periods, while proclaiming to be spiritually mature, we show a double-faced character. This is what James speaks of as "blessing" and "cursing" from the same mouth. Our words are a good thermometer to measure our spiritual temperature.

Just as a good tree is judged by the kind of fruit it bears, so a Christian is measured by the words he uses. James asks, "Does a stream pour forth from the same opening fresh water and brackish? Can a fig tree, my brethren, yield olives, or a grapevine figs?" (3:11, 12). Jesus used the same analogy in speaking of false teachers (Matt. 7:15-20). James strengthens his point by saying that evil words, if used regularly and consistently, are a good indication that a person's heart is not right. Words will be a basis for divine judgment (Matt. 12:37), but they are also a basis for human evaluation. How important therefore that we watch our words and learn to "speak the truth in love" to our neighbors (Eph. 4:15, 25).

James gives his antidote for the evils of the tongue in chapter 1 (vv. 19-21), in the form of three terse yet powerful commands. He says, "Let every man be quick to hear, slow to speak, slow to anger" (v. 19). Anger is one of James's chief targets because anger is most often expressed verbally. Most people vent their anger with words, though some may be more violent and do physical harm. Too often, however, angry words do as much harm as physical attack. While children may repeat the quip "Sticks and stones will break my bones, but names will never hurt me," it is still true that we can and do hurt people with our tongue. Perhaps those who are closest to us feel it most.

First, says James, we should be *quick to listen*. Most arguments would never get started if people would listen in the beginning. Second, James says it is necessary to be *slow to speak*. This is essential to fulfill his first command. We could listen better if we learned to hold our tongue. Too often we're thinking of our next word instead of listening to the other person. The Chinese have a good practice. They do not reply immediately after being spoken to. They pause to think through what has been said. To them you haven't really listened if you reply immediately.

The Preacher said, "Be not rash with your mouth . . . let your words be few," and "a dream comes with much business, and a fool's voice with many words" (Eccles. 5:2, 3). One of Solomon's proverbs reads, "When words are many, transgression is not lacking, but he who restrains his lips is prudent" (Prov. 10:19). Third, James says we should be *slow to anger*. If we practice the first two commands this will come easier.

James's final thought centers in the positive power of God's Word to change behavior. "Filthiness and wickedness" must go so that the "implanted word" can be received. The key to speaking words that build up and encourage is to be saturated with truth, good thoughts, and the words of God. God's Word, "which is able to save your souls" (1:21), is the word Jesus said was

60

"spirit and life" (John 6:63). When a person's mind is filled with truth, he will speak the truth and be a "doer of the word" (James 1:22). Only in this sense will the tongue be tamed.

LET'S DISCUSS

1. Why did James warn against becoming teachers (3:1)? Does this refer to all positions of leadership? Why is the use of words important for those in positions of leadership?

2. How does James describe the nature of the tongue? Why is the tongue untamable? What controls the tongue?

3. If being in a position of leadership brings stricter judgment, does this mean that a person who avoids leadership gets off easier? Why or why not?

4. Give some examples how "blessing and cursing" come from the same mouth (3:10). How does this affect a person's relation to his family? to his church? to the world?

5. In what way do our words reveal our character? How far should we go in taking a person's words at face value?

6. Do you think God's judgment of "every careless word" (Matt. 12:36-37) is extreme? Why or why not? What is a careless word? Is this a reference to "small talk"? What about jesting and humor?

7. How can Christians learn to control their tongues? How does genuine listening help? How do we develop listening skills?

8. Do "Freudian slips" have significance? In what sense do they reveal a person's real thinking? What are the dangers of making too much of them?

9. How can we avoid hypocritical speech? How should we confront a person who speaks falsely?
10. Is there any way we can test our speech to discern whether what we say is acceptable to God? How can we measure the impact of our words on other people?

7. Who Is the Wise One?

"Who is wise and understanding among you? By his good life let him show his works in the meekness of wisdom. But if you have bitter jealousy and selfish ambition in your hearts, do not boast and be false to the truth. This wisdom is not such as comes down from above, but is earthly, unspiritual, devilish. For where jealousy and selfish ambition exist, there will be disorder and every vile practice. But the wisdom from above is first pure, then peaceable, gentle, open to reason, full of mercy and good fruits, without uncertainty or insincerity. And the harvest of righteousness is sown in peace by those who make peace" (James 3:13-18).

Wisdom cannot be judged or measured on the basis of knowledge alone. An astute politician, a learned scientist, or a well-trained technician could amass considerable knowledge and yet be unwise. No direct correlation exists between knowledge and wisdom. Scientific facts do not necessarily produce wisdom, though facts may aid one's judgment.

Recently newspapers reported that the FBI was searching for a man who had a Ph.D. degree from Stanford University. He was accused of placing bombs in bank safety deposit boxes. In a suburb of Chicago an M.D. was convicted of raping a patient after giving her drugs. In Washington, a long-time congressman was accused of mail fraud. Author Clifford Irving thought he could successfully peddle a faked autobiography of billionaire Howard Hughes.

All of these men had considerable knowledge—knowledge they used in their schemes: the one to destroy property, the other for lustful gratification, the last two for money. Yet their knowledge was used unwisely. They were knowledgeable, but not wise.

Does this mean that knowledge and wisdom are antithetical? By no means. It simply means that knowledge is no substitute for wisdom. Wisdom stems from a person's character. When it is correctly expressed, it makes the best use of knowledge, but it is not dependent on it.

James talks about how wisdom is expressed. He divides wisdom into two categories based on what motivates men. He proclaims that wisdom can have either a good or an evil source. Wisdom from above stems from good motivations within a person; wisdom from below issues from evil motives. Wisdom that has only a human motivational source expresses itself in seeking personal gain.

James declares that bitter jealousy motivated some believers. He does not elaborate on what caused the jealousy or the nature of the jealousy. It had developed into a bitter rivalry. Any activity or show of cleverness that sprang from this attitude was something, according to James, that didn't have heavenly motivation. The Spirit of God had no part in producing the jealousy. In Galatians 5:22-23, the apostle Paul says that the fruit of the spirit is love . . . peace . . . longsuffering—all opposites of bitter jealousy.

Coupled with jealousy of others is selfish ambition. This kind of motivation cripples a Christian in relationship to true wisdom. Selfish ambition tramples over others in much the same way as bitter jealousy does—in total disregard of others. But in condemning selfish ambition, the apostle is not condemning all ambition. In verse 13 he even says that wisdom and understanding are shown by works. Paul says in Colossians 3:23, "Whatever your task, work heartily, as serving the Lord." Ambition that is geared to glorifying God is a healthy personality trait. How great it would be if all Christians were known for their ambition to glorify God and to strengthen others in their faith. A wise man who is motivated by God will not be guilty of self-assertion and arrogance, but will be a gentle, humble, hard worker.

James warns that "where jealousy and selfish ambition exist, there will be disorder and every vile practice" (3:16). This is natural because, whenever these personality traits are expressed, there will be constant struggle between individuals for supremacy. One will try to outdo the other, and many resort to the most depraved practices.

James however does present an optimistic side to the issue. The wisdom which comes from above portrays the characteristics of Jesus Christ. When such wisdom resides in the believer, it will be manifested in his contacts with others—both believers and nonbelievers.

Wisdom that has heavenly motivation—which expresses the mind of God through human decisions—is called "frame of mind" by Bible expositor Manford Gutzke. He doesn't see wisdom as a kind of mystical entity which invades a man's personality. Rather, it is a wisdom that is the expression of an astute, proper frame of mind in any given situation.

If our frame of mind is dominated by the Holy Spirit, the thoughts of our minds will be in harmony with the mind of Christ. To this end we are challenged by Paul in Philippians 4:8, "Finally, brethren, whatever is true, whatever is honorable, whatever is just, whatever is pure, whatever is lovely, whatever is gracious, if there is any excellence, if there is anything worthy of praise, think about these things."

Both James and Paul emphasize purity of thought. This is in contrast to the selfishness and bitter jealousy about which James writes. The wisdom that originates with God is pure first of all because God is pure. It is pure because it is unselfish and because it has a delicate sensibility to anything that would pollute the decision-making process.

The frame of mind that is God oriented and God dominated is peaceable. It possesses itself and expresses itself in self-controlled temperament toward others.

We have much need for improvement in the peace department. Too often we've been known for our contentiousness. We've lambasted our opposition with verbal rockets. We've torn down our enemies with fiery words. We've forgotten the words of James, "The wisdom from above is . . . peaceable."

During the past half-century a strong battle has raged between the fundamentalists and the liberals. Those who have proclaimed the love of God the loudest, even quoting the many verses about Christian love from the New Testament, have seemed to show the least love. The liberals, whose motivations have been from the humanistic side, often have demonstrated more love than the fundamentalists who use the love of God as a weapon to destroy their opponents. How different from the spirit advocated by the apostle James!

As Cardinal Newman once told a friend, "You have discharged your olive branch with a catapult." That's the impression many Christians give to the world, especially when their declarations of peace are more aggressive than their declarations of war.

We need to ask, Do my verbal barrages make another person more contentious and aggressive? Am I showing contention and aggressiveness? Am I communicating or am I simply fighting? Is my profession of brotherly love a screen for inner animosities?

Jesus, though He stood firm against sin and had confrontations with people around Him, knew the secret of living at peace with others. People sensed His love toward them. They sensed He had the character to back up His claims. And though He could easily put the responsibility for evil on the evildoers, He compassionately extended His mercy toward them.

James says that we express the mind of our Lord best when we are gentle, full of mercy and good fruits. Mercy and compassion need to invade our personalities as we look out toward our world. We need a gentle attitude toward the downtrodden, toward those who have little or no means to help themselves, and toward those who commit wrongs against us.

"It is equity," said Aristotle, "to pardon human failings, and to look to the lawgiver and not to the law, to the spirit and not to the letter, to the intention and not to the action, to the whole and not to the part, to the character of the actor in the long run and not to the present moment, to remember good rather than evil, and good that one has received rather than good that one has done, to put up with injurious treatment, to wish to settle a matter by words rather than by deeds, to prefer arbitration to judgment in the courts." If the virtue of gentleness is alive and active in this manner, much injustice would disappear from our society.

Probably one of the most glaring lacks of churchy wisdom in the past, and one of the most needed virtues of the present, is what James refers to as an openness to reason. Many Christians adopt a black/white attitude toward life. This distorts their reason. For them, everything is an either/or situation. Some conservatives (political as well as theological) fail to see the other person's point of view, giving the impression that they have a corner on God's wisdom.

To be open-minded on contemporary issues is a threat to many people. They can't tolerate positions other than their own. To do so is an attack on their narrow, we-have-the-answers approach to life. To say they don't know all the answers threatens the foundations upon which they have built their systems of belief. There is no place for alternate positions.

Open-mindedness, however, is not synonymous with compromise. In fact, it can be one of the strongest fortifications for true faith. A faith that can examine all the possibilities and adhere to those that are in harmony with Scripture will be a more vital faith. Open-mindedness helps a person understand all the facts and facets of a subject without being threatened. It also helps the individual to communicate his faith to those who have views not quite like his own.

During the past decade many moral, ethical, and social problems have been thrust upon us. We've had many opportunities but haven't done much about them. It is difficult to come up with absolute answers, as some Christians demand. Even Christians disagree on such subjects as abortion, birth control, capital punishment, genetic control. Can a person take an absolute position on such subjects? As concerned Christians we must be open-minded to new possibilities that may help solve some of the pressing problems. New research, new study methods of the Bible, new applications of moral principles will help us match our faith with our actions.

This is not in conflict with James's view that our frame of mind ought to be without uncertainty and insincerity. We must hold fast to all those truths that are clearly set forth in Scripture. We can be absolutely certain about doctrines and principles which are plainly stated in the Bible. It would show uncertainty and insincerity to proclaim principles or doctrines that cannot be supported by Scripture. Open-mindedness is opposed to self-assertive and dogmatic obstinacy—even when it seems safer to adopt doctrinaire, cut-and-dried positions.

Who is the wise one? According to James, it is the person who shows God's wisdom through his "good life" (3:13). We must put ourselves in a place of value to Christ and to the world; we must come out of our cloisterlike existence and enter the world with the frame of mind of Christ. We must be vulnerable, even if it means abandoning a cherished idea in order to proclaim God's wisdom in a "pure, gentle, peaceable, open-minded, merciful, fruitful, sincere, and certain" manner of life. This is truly wise living!

LET'S DISCUSS

1. What is the difference between wisdom and knowledge? Does wisdom depend on knowledge? In what ways?

2. Can a person improve his "WQ" (wisdom quotient; cf. the expression "IQ")? Does a person become wiser by practice or is wisdom innate? Explain.

3. What is a wise decision? How does James distinguish between a wise decision and a poor one?

4. In I Corinthians 1:20 it says that God has made foolish the wisdom of the world. Explain. Of what value is worldly wisdom?

5. In Luke 16:8 it says that the sons of this world are wiser than the children of light. How can this be? Should Christians be wiser than unbelievers? In what sense?

6. What criteria can we use to determine whether we are depending on worldly wisdom or wisdom from above? How does one know when God has given wisdom as promised in James 1:5?

7. What is the relationship between common sense and wisdom?

8. Since James says that we should ask for wisdom, why not make one request for this as a permanent gift? Why should we continually pray for wisdom? Does such asking imply that wisdom is limited to each situation? Explain.

9. Discuss some specific situations in which you sensed a fresh influx of wisdom from above.

8. Problems with Passions

"What causes wars, and what causes fightings among you? Is it not your passions that are at war in your members? You desire and do not have; so you kill. And you covet and cannot obtain; so you fight and wage war. You do not have, because you do not ask. You ask and do not receive, because you ask wrongly, to spend it on your passions. Unfaithful creatures! Do you not know that friendship with the world is enmity with God? Therefore whoever wishes to be a friend of the world makes himself an enemy of God. Or do you suppose it is in vain that the scripture says, 'He yearns jealously over the spirit which he has made to dwell in us'? But he gives more grace; therefore it says, 'God opposes the proud, but gives grace to the humble.' Submit yourselves therefore to God. Resist the devil and he will flee from you. Draw near to God and he will draw near to you. Cleanse your hands, you sinners, and purify your hearts, you men of double mind. Be

wretched and mourn and weep. Let your laughter be turned to mourning and your joy to dejection. Humble yourselves before the Lord and he will exalt you" (James 4:1-10).

Thousands of books have been based on the conflicts between men. Authors use conflicts to entertain men's minds. Others attempt to explain why one person rises against another. Page after page is filled with excuses or reasons to justify man's murderous behavior. Some explanations seem plausible; others only fortify the fact that man's basic tendencies are toward evil.

James presents the root causes of human conflicts with the terseness of a telegram. These conflicts, he says, are caused by individual passions. Once a person conquers the problem of his evil passions, he learns the peace of God which inspires peaceful relationships with other people. But how does a person conquer his passions?

The King James Version translates the word for passions as "lusts." In our day the word *lust* usually refers to illicit sexual passion. It never has a good connotation. Lusts or evil passions have as their roots the desire for pleasurable experiences beyond the normal experiences of life. Lust cares little for the needs or feelings of others.

It is natural to seek a certain amount of pleasure. Modern man devotes much of his time, energy, money, interest, and enthusiasm to this end. There is nothing wrong with getting personal enjoyment from living, but pleasures often war against each other within a person. Peter told his readers "to abstain from the passions of the flesh that wage war against your soul" (I Peter 2:11).

He knew that evil passions corrupted the personality of the individual. Such passions prevented a man from doing what he was created to do—to obey and serve God.

The fierce desire to have the good things of life often causes a person to trample over others. Passions are centered in selfish desires for gratification, not in altruistic attitudes to help others.

There is no better word to describe evil passions than the word "lust." Lust is like atomic energy within the human personality. It is a deceiving power within the person. It embraces a vast range of base desires and emotions. The Bible never pictures lust as good. Lust includes evil ambition, avarice, unlawful yearnings, covetousness, jealousy, resentment, anger, spite, envying, strife. Such passions, which begin in the heart of the individual, are soon expressed outwardly. And when vented toward others, they cause inward struggles, quarrels among friends, and strife in the church community.

James says that we don't have what we desire because we don't ask God and because, when we do ask God, we ask for the wrong reasons. There is a relationship between asking and receiving. James echoes the words of Jesus, "Ask, and it will be given you; seek, and you will find; knock, and it will be opened to you" (Matt. 7:7). The trouble is, we don't bother asking. We don't pray enough or with enough desire. Many Christians only pray in emergencies—and never discover whether their requests are in line with the will of God. When Jesus said we should ask for anything in His name, with the promise that we would receive it from God, He assumed an underlying state of a right relationship to God. How can one be sure he has this underlying relationship to the

Father if he makes no effort to contact God on a regular basis?

If a person doesn't have this day-to-day relationship with God, he won't know what is in harmony with God's will for him when he prays. Rather, as James forcefully states, when such a person prays, "you ask and do not receive, because you ask wrongly, to spend it on your passions."

A person whose religion is only a get-for-himself relationship to God, will ask God mainly for those things that bring pleasure to himself; things "to spend on his passions."

God does not hear such prayers because their ulterior motive is merely to have more time and strength to spend satisfying personal desires. God doesn't listen to prayers that ask Him to satisfy one's covetousness, ambition, and love of luxury. These are an abomination to the Lord.

The prayers God hears include the open cries of the righteous (Ps. 34:15); those uttered out of truthful hearts (Ps. 145:18); the cries of penitents (Luke 18:14); those which are in line with the will of God (I John 5:14).

When a man doesn't pray or when he doesn't pray in the will of God, he eventually turns to the world to satisfy his passions. James clearly points this out when he follows the statement about prayer with the words, "Do you not know that friendship with the world is enmity with God? Therefore whoever wishes to be a friend of the world makes himself an enemy of God" (4:4).

A Christian cannot divide his loyalties between God and the world. He cannot please both at the same time.

Jesus says, "You cannot serve God and mammon" (Matt. 6:24). While this had specific reference to serving money, Jesus knew that money represented the world system. One cannot seek self-gratification and the love of pleasure and still maintain loyalty to God. Once a man makes a deliberate choice to satisfy himself, he automatically turns his back on God.

Many Christians have propagated the legalistic heresy of limiting worldliness to participation in certain games, seeking bodily pleasures, or attending certain public amusements. They make comfortable "we don't do" lists. One cannot make such listings, even though a person living in a harmonious relationship to God may consider such things outside the activities he believes are pleasing to God. If a list of worldly activities could be compiled, who would have the final authority for putting the last item on the list? Would a rigid adherence to these "don't" laws guarantee a right relationship to God? Would such a list bring a person closer to Christ?

Spirituality does not consist in a rigid and conscientious observation of external rules. It consists in having a right spirit, of living in a sensitive relationship to and in a constant fellowship with God. A spiritual person has purposed to do the will of God in all things, regardless of the cost.

The criteria for worldliness center in the attitudes of an individual, not in his activities. One can abstain from certain traditionally designated worldly activities and still be quite worldly. Worldliness consists in one's attitude toward the world and toward God. We ought to list the following as marks of worldliness: not allowing God to have His proper place of authority in our lives; letting self dominate in the decisions of life; putting material

75

things before spiritual pursuits; showing partiality toward people of other races; and excluding the poor from church fellowship.

A worldly person does little to win God's approval. He simply lives to please himself or those around him. At the same time he pays little attention to the fact that God condemns his approach to life. He has little sense of the evils of personal sin. He maintains an I-don't-care position about whether his attitudes and actions are right or wrong in the sight of God. Along with this carefree attitude toward sin, the worldly person gives little thought to the idea of facing God as his judge.

The worldly person does little to bring himself into an intimate, continuous contact with God. He might go through religious exercises in church or go through the motions of a personal devotional period, but he accomplishes little in communications with the Lord. Rarely is he concerned whether his words get through to God. As we have stated before, friendship with the world is enmity with God. The worldly person does not get close to God because to do so condemns his actions. His basic life style is incompatible with God's will, for enmity exists between God and worldliness.

Just as we have seen in the opening verses of this chapter, fightings and satisfying evil passions along with other worldly attitudes are soul-destroying qualities. Man has no remedy in himself, nor can he reform himself into being nonworldly. He might subdue some of his worst passions, but ultimately he will show his true nature.

Man is helpless unless he takes the prescription offered by James in verses 7-10. Here James lists actions that bring about a right relationship to God, that assure tranquility of spirit, and that cause the inner wars to cease. He says, "Submit yourselves therefore to God." That's just the opposite of a worldly attitude, for it forces a man to relinquish the controls of his life into the hands of God. It makes surrender of the will an active endeavor, not merely the words of a song or an ideal. "Resist the devil" comes next. Turn your back on Satan, not on God. Make sure that this isn't only a mental rejection of Satan, but also a rejection of those acts and attitudes of rebellion against the authority of the Lord. To resist implies more than passive resistance; it calls for an active battle.

"Draw near to God"—in a mental and willful attitude. Keep your thoughts in line with an active relationship with God. Think upon His person. Follow His ways. "Cleanse your hands ... and purify your hearts." Take care of any cleansing that is necessary. Couple this with an inward personality that has been transformed and cleansed by the blood of Christ. "Mourn and weep." Maintain a sensitivity about personal rebellion and sin. Let it cause tears of repentance. And finally, "Humble yourselves before the Lord." Evaluate yourself correctly in the sight of God and of others. In doing this, God will exalt you and bring great grace into your life. You'll live at peace with Him, with yourself, with others.

LET'S DISCUSS

1. Give some of the reasons why people strive and fight. Why are these in conflict with the Bible? Are any human reasons for conflict valid?

2. How do we distinguish between the sin of covetousness and a natural desire to have pleasant things and surroundings? Is it wrong to have such natural desires?

3. How do you know when you are praying in the right manner? How can you tell when you are asking simply to satisfy your passions? Should you ask God for good things in life?

4. How can you tell when you are lining up on God's side and against the world? How do you protect yourself from worldliness and still communicate to the world?

5. What is worldliness? Is it limited to amusements and pleasures or does it include attitudes about people and things? How does this kind of worldliness express itself among church people?

6. Is there a sense in which it is proper to be a friend of the world? Should a Christian maintain friendship with unbelievers? How far should this friendship go?

7. What does the word "grace" as used in James 4:6 mean? What is humility? Why does God hate pride?

8. In what sense does the Lord "exalt" us because of our humility? How does this exalting differ from the self-exalting pride that God opposes?

9. In the light of James 4:7-10, how can you avoid a stereotyped devotional life? How can you keep your prayers fresh, honest, and vital?

10. How do you resist the devil? What do we mean when we speak of the devil? Do we mean direct encounter? How can you validate encounters with the devil?

9. Who Made You A Judge?

"Do not speak evil against one another, brethren. He that speaks evil against a brother or judges his brother, speaks evil against the law and judges the law. But if you judge the law, you are not a doer of the law but a judge. There is one lawgiver and judge, he who is able to save and to destroy. But who are you that you judge your neighbor?" (James 4:11, 12).

You have every right in the world to evaluate the personalities and actions of others. Neither James nor Jesus had any prohibitions against evaluating people when they said, "Do not judge." One would be totally at a loss in establishing friendships, hiring employees, getting adequate work done by associates, or predicting how others would react under stress if he did not evaluate other people.

Not long ago an executive hired a new secretary. She filled out the necessary applications and appeared to be very capable for the position. Being a Christian gentleman, the executive gave her every opportunity to prove

79

herself. He studied her personality and work habits along with the work she produced. He took into account that she was a new Christian and that he could be instrumental in helping strengthen her relationship to Christ. But as the weeks went by, he discovered she wasn't capable of producing the quality of work for which she was hired. There were also some definite deficiencies in her character that hindered healthy relationships with others in the office. Before the first month was up, he had judged (or if you prefer, evaluated) her work and found that it did not meet the level of competence he expected from his secretary. He faced the unpleasant task of communicating his evaluation to her and telling her to seek other employment.

A young seminary graduate went to a pastorate in a small midwestern town. He discovered that the people had few convictions. They practiced what they pleased—and no outsider was going to change them. The young man continually presented Scriptural views on Christian living, both from its positive and negative aspects. He tried to lead the people into greater commitment to Jesus Christ.

The reaction of the congregation was almost unanimous—except for a couple of saints who rejected the others' attitudes and rejoiced in their new preacher's stand for the Word of God. But the others, who didn't want any young upstart of a preacher saying they needed to change their ways of living to please God, cried, "Pastor, who made you a judge?"

A neighboring pastor jokingly told the young pastor to return to his people and say, "I'm not a judge; I'm simply a fruit inspector! Didn't Jesus say, 'By their fruits you shall know them'?"

One needs to establish quite clearly in his own thinking the difference between evaluating another's personality and performance and judging that person unjustly. Sometimes it is easy to make this distinction. Sometimes there appears to be an exceedingly fine line between legitimate evaluation of another's personality and performance and judging or criticizing a person unjustly.

The ability to see into the character of others is to be desired and cultivated. Being able to discern the weaknesses and strengths of another person, to have psychological perception concerning a person are assets every person should develop. The study of human nature is a valid science, as valid as the study of theology. One cannot minister to the whole man if he lacks understanding of who man is. The failure to understand the character of people around us is nothing about which anyone should boast. Failing to understand and discern the character of others is the basis of most mistrust and strife among people.

Jesus probably is the best example of a person who evaluated the characters of those around Him. On several occasions He predicted people's actions before they happened. The Gospel writers tell us that He knew what was in man. He challenged the attitudes of the religious people before they spoke. He confounded His listeners by revealing things about them that only they themselves knew. An excellent example of this power was our Lord's encounter with the woman at the well. He evaluated her character so explicitly that she ran and told her friends to come and see a man who told her everything she ever did. Surely our Master wouldn't condemn our evaluation of others when He made such evaluations continually. Giving the believer some of His personal power surely included this ability. A wise person will always be able to penetrate deep into the personality of his fellows.

The study of psychology is based on the premise that we can and should evaluate the personalities and performances of people around us. By analyzing what people do, by probing into some of the reasons behind their actions, by learning how often such actions will be repeated, we learn how people behave.

We classify people according to their mental capacities, oddities, and abnormalities. After psychological evaluations, medical science can properly treat abnormalities and bring people back to acceptable patterns of behavior.

What were James and Jesus really talking about when they said, "Judge not"? And why is there so much confusion about what judging is or is not? How can a person avoid this confusion?

First, consider the character of the person who is doing the judging. Has he placed himself in the role of the final authority on a specific issue? Is he comparing the other person to himself or with what he imagines to be the perfect ideal? If so, he does not express charity toward the person being judged. Rather, he is being condemnatory. We are constantly competing to get ahead of others, so there's always a strong temptation to downgrade others—perhaps out of fear that they may take our place. Verbal blasts at others sometimes prove most effective in pushing us ahead. Both James and Jesus warn us against this, for it is self-defeating. A judge often has two standards of conduct: one standard for judging his neighbor—one that is critical and condemnatory; and another standard for himself—one that condones inferior or wrong behavior.

It has been said that the person who loudly and continually goes about condemning certain activities in others often has the same faults within himself. Although this is not always the case, it can be true. The faultfinder diverts some attention away from his personal faults by concentrating on and broadcasting the faults of his neighbors.

The judging person usually uses a microscope to examine the faults of others. Under the microscope, faults are exaggerated and can give the viewer only a glimpse at a minute portion of what is being viewed. The whole cannot be considered. Likewise, when a person takes this approach toward others, he usually does not consider the whole person. He presents an exaggerated picture of one individual fault.

Contrariwise, this person usually looks through the wrong end of a telescope at his own faults. They are diminished to the extent that he does not see them as faults.

How much better to use the microscope on oneself and the inverted telescope on others. Unfortunately, in our competitive world, this isn't likely to come about. Only through the infusion of the grace of God will we be able to reverse the method by which we judge others.

Take, for instance, one man accusing another of unkindness. He might see another man punishing his children and conclude that the person is extremely cruel. His microscopic approach of arguing from one speck of evidence to the whole is an unkindness in itself. His desire to show that the other man is cruel is an unkindness. If he broadcasts his conclusions on the basis of one encounter, he becomes guilty of the same offense. Yet his inverted telescopic view of himself makes him consider himself virtuous. How easy it is for people to deceive themselves.

The Living Bible translates "speaking evil" as "backbiting." This means derogatory speaking behind another's back when he is not present to defend himself. Backbiting goes far beyond the bounds of legitimate evaluation. Backbiting passes judgment without either having the opportunity of knowing or even desiring to know the truth. The person listening to these verbal blasts usually cannot repeat them word for word and thus gets the wrong impression. Usually that is exactly what the backbiter wants.

James says that the person who judges others harshly actually sets himself in opposition to the law of God which says that people ought to love one another. By his judging, he makes himself a judge of the law—claiming that the law doesn't apply in his case at that time. Whenever a person speaks evil of the law, as James states, by breaking it he opposes God—the originator of the law. When a person doesn't practice what the law says, he becomes a self-styled authority. He then operates outside the realm of God's rule for his life. And whether you are a believer or an unbeliever, such an attitude eliminates God from your life at the point at which you supplant God as the final judge of others. Such judging usurps the place of judgment that belongs to the Lord alone.

James says it is not for the believer to pass judgment on whether the law of God is right or wrong. Our task is to obey all of God's laws. In this respect, the law of love keeps us from unjustly criticizing others. Our obedience to the law of love allows us to properly evaluate the lives of others. But we must leave the ultimate condemnation or praise of their lives in the hands of the Lord. Our obedience to the law of love will motivate us to be merciful toward others, even as the Lord is merciful to us.

LET'S DISCUSS

1. What Scripture verses indicate that God is the final judge of men's characters? Did Jesus judge people when He was on earth? In what ways? How did this differ from unjust, critical judgment?

2. The study of psychology leads a person to analyze the personalities of others. How does this kind of analysis differ from judging in the biblical sense? How does psychological understanding fit into the pattern of a Christian approach to others?

3. Are there dangers in psychology for Christians? How can one guard against these dangers?

4. What are the values of psychology for Christians? How can psychological knowledge help them become less critical of others?

5. Does the idea of love toward others limit our right to evaluate their behavior and beliefs?

6. What difficulties do we have when evaluating the personalities and performances of others? Give examples and tell how to guard against these possibilities.

7. If we know, on the basis of biblical truths, that a fellow Christian is living in sin, what should be our

attitude toward that person? How should we express this to him? to others?

8. If we knew of a situation in which a person was criticized unjustly, what should we do to correct the injustice? Why should we get involved?

9. How can a Christian maintain a Scriptural attitude and keep from being severe toward those who do not follow Scripture? How far should we go in judging and evaluating ourselves?

10. Can you state God's judgment upon certain attitudes and actions without being judgmental yourself? How can you express the love of Christ toward those whose way of life is opposed to the love you show?

10. Practical Atheism

"Come now, you who say, 'Today or tomorrow we will go into such and such a town and spend a year there and trade and get gain'; whereas you do not know about tomorrow. What is your life? For you are a mist that appears for a little time and then vanishes. Instead you ought to say, 'If the Lord wills, we shall live and we shall do this or that.' As it is, you boast in your arrogance. All such boasting is evil. Whoever knows what is right to do and fails to do it, for him it is sin" (James 4:13-17).

The height of man's arrogance becomes more evident as he tries to build a world without reference to God. We are experiencing this phenomenon in our day, but it is nothing new. Since earliest recorded history mankind has tried to organize life apart from a divine being. Some have done it openly, proclaiming that God did not exist; or if they had doubts about His reality, they asserted that it was impossible to know whether He actually did exist.

There are various kinds of atheists: those who openly deny God's existence—pure atheists; those who don't know if He exists—agnostics; those who live as if He didn't exist—practical atheists. This latter type is by far the largest group. They probably would not consider themselves atheists as commonly defined; and if you asked, they probably would say they believed in God—at least in some kind of a god.

In recent times we have been hearing a new twist to this old idea. Theologians, in the name of the Christian religion, have proclaimed a "christian atheism." The death-of-God theology was an attempt to establish a religious system that retained the timeless elements of Christianity (authenticity, being, freedom) without holding the traditional doctrines of a transcendent God and a supernatural Christ. They proclaimed that the concept of God had no meaning for modern man. Therefore they concluded that new religious expressions and ideas were needed to attract men to a "new being."

One of the bywords of modern theological thinking has been "secular religion." Another was "religionless Christianity." This was Bonhoeffer's not-so-easy-to-understand concept that the best way to communicate the gospel might be through secular channels and non-religious language. Bonhoeffer's idea mushroomed and was adopted by the radical theologians who finally proclaimed the "death of God." They devised a humanistic religion that was supposed to meet the needs of a humanistic society. The primary problem, however, with trying to establish a *secularity* with religious values is keeping it from becoming no more than an irreligious *secularism.*

A mood of secularism dominates our culture and even

endangers evangelical churches. Many Christians, who would never tolerate modern theology in their thinking, have, perhaps unwittingly, fallen victim to the secular mood. They live their lives no differently than their non-Christian neighbors. They strive for material possessions with as much fervor as avid materialists. They adopt current ethical standards without regard to biblical ethical principles. While they give lip-service to God on Sunday, they make sure their children get some religious education. Though nominally orthodox in their beliefs, there is hardly any evidence in their manner of life that shows they have been transformed by the grace of God through Jesus Christ.

This is the heart of the problem about which James speaks in the last part of chapter 4. He challenges man's boastful arrogance and pride. He begins by showing that man's knowledge is limited. Man cannot know the future. He cannot say with any certainty, "Today or tomorrow we will go into such and such a town and spend a year there and trade and get gain" (v. 13).

Life is not that stable. The stock market can go up for months, and tumble down in days. Tranquility and peace can be disrupted over a small incident. Sickness, disease, or disability can crush a rising career in a short time. Friends can turn against you; loved ones can let you down; employers can transfer you to another part of the country; life can become drudgery and failure. We can't be absolutely sure of our earthly future. All the planning in the world can be rendered useless by one mistake. That's life. Solomon said, "Do not boast about tomorrow, for you do not know what a day may bring forth" (Prov. 27:1).

The best men can do is to plan wisely for the future and hope that God's goodness will allow those plans to be fulfilled. At worst, our planning can dull our sense of dependence on God. We can feel so secure we forget God gave us what we have. The rich farmer enlarged his storehouses to rest in a false security, but God thwarted his plans when He demanded his life (Luke 12:19, 20).

A rich man died and a friend asked, "How much did he leave?" The answer was, "Everything!" The writer of Ecclesiastes complained of "an evil" that "lies heavy upon men: a man to whom God gives wealth, possessions, and honor, so that he lacks nothing of all he desires, yet God does not give him power to enjoy them, but a stranger enjoys them; this is vanity" (Eccles. 6:1-2). How pitiable to spend one's life without enjoying the fruit of one's labors.

To James, the explanation is very simple. *Life is short.* "What is your life? For you are a mist that appears for a little time and then vanishes" (4:14). At most the average man lives "threescore and ten"—just about what life expectancy is today, thanks to modern technology and medicine. But even at that, life is as a mist. We have no guarantee that tomorrow will come.

Man recognizes that life is short, so he tries all types of methods to extend life indefinitely. Magic potions, secret rites, and all sorts of curious schemes have been devised in the attempt to make man immortal. The most ambitious in our day is "cryogenics"—freezing a person before cellular death with the prospect of reanimating him sometime in the future. A few people have been frozen immediately after being pronounced medically dead, in hopes that this will work. Apart from the ethical, social, and economic problems, this idea overlooks the ultimate facts of aging and death.

90

Probably this great interest in solving the problem of overcoming death stems from man's failure to face the real problems of life. He tends to deal only with the symptoms. The real problem of death is a spiritual one while the person is alive. Freezing bodies is simply attacking symptoms, not the causes. When men can accept the biblical concept of sin and the reality of Jesus Christ as the Savior from sin, then they will solve the problems of immortality. Then life—as long as they possess it—will be worthwhile. "For to me to live is Christ, and to die is gain" (Phil. 1:21).

James teaches the sovereignty of God. He says that instead of living as if God does not exist, saying to ourselves, "I am free to do what I want, when I want, and nobody has anything to say about it," we ought to say, "If the Lord wills, we shall live and we shall do this or that" (4:15).

When James says this, is he asking us to add another cliché to our vocabulary? Is he telling us to add "If it be Your will" to our prayers when we don't really mean it? These are good questions because, frankly, it is rather tiring to hear the phrase used so often in pseudopious ways. People say, "I'll be there, Lord willing" and get into the habit of saying it as a kind of pious formula. It comes to mean little to those who hear it and less to the person using it. But James is not saying that we should repeat the phrase as some kind of guarantee of spirituality.

What James is talking about goes to the depths of a person's thinking about life. He is talking about a God consciousness that controls a person's entire being and thought processes. It is the ability of approaching any thought, deed, or decision with the awareness that God has the ultimate "okay" and authority. It is recognizing

91

God's place in our lives. We acknowledge that His will is more important than our own and that we cannot bend His will to ours. He is the sovereign, final authority. Again, Solomon's insight sums up the proper attitude: "Do not rely on your own insight. In all your ways acknowledge him, and he will make straight your paths" (Prov. 3:5, 6).

James looks upon the we-can-do-anything-we-please attitude as basically boastful arrogance (4:16), which is evil. "Pride goes before destruction, and a haughty spirit before a fall" (Prov. 16:18). Humility of spirit is a grace that should characterize every Christian—especially in his basic attitude toward living. Humility is best expressed in a person's attitude toward his use of time and resources.

False humility puts on a show of poverty or moderation, but is without a real expression of quiet faithfulness to God. Boastful humility usually shouts at you whenever you come in contact with it. Self-demeaning and humiliating acts often reveal an extreme arrogance that is miles apart from real humility. Boasting of one's humility, according to James, is sin, no matter how subtly done.

True humility does not "boast of tomorrow." Nor does it glibly use clichés like "God willing." Real humility lives with the realization that God holds the strings and that "we ain't going nowhere if he lets go." True humility accepts each day as a gift from God and values time as an opportunity to serve rather than as an outlet for pleasure.

After showing that living without acknowledging God's direction in our lives is nothing more than sinful arrogance, James takes his argument a step further. He says, "Whoever knows what is right to do and fails to do it, for him it is sin" (4:17). Relating this to what preceded it, James emphasizes that it is right (or good) to openly seek God's direction. To fail in this is to omit an important part of Christian living. If our everyday manner of living is no different than that of the average unbeliever, we are denying God's effectiveness in our lives. Omitting God from our lives is the greatest sin.

Verse 17 carries with it an important principle for Christians. It continues one step further the theme that James talked about in chapter 3. James warned against becoming a teacher because the responsibility carried with it a greater strictness in the day of judgment. In verse 17 James states that knowledge of what is good and right puts a person in a more vulnerable position toward sin. Does this mean then that there is a sense in which ignorance can be excused? No, for we are all "without excuse" (Rom. 1:20). What it does mean is that certain behavior or lack of it is unjustified in the light of our awareness of what is good.

We are familiar with the apathy and indifference toward doing good to others evidenced in our society. We hear reports of people being mugged in broad daylight without anyone lifting a finger to help. One man lay unconscious beside an expressway for several hours before someone came to help. Later motorists said that they passed by, thinking someone else would stop and help. They knew someone should stop and help, but "passed by on the other side." Jesus told of this same behavior and condemned it in the story of the Good Samaritan.

One of the evidences of spiritual maturity is the growing recognition that certain personal behavior no longer can be tolerated. As we grow from "babes in Christ" (I Peter 2:2) to mature Christians (Eph. 4:13, 14), we are made aware of attitudes and behavior that no longer can be ignored. Such attitudes and actions become sin when our deeper knowledge of God and greater sensitivity about the consequences of our actions no longer permit us to harbor these things.

LET'S DISCUSS

1. In what sense are many people "practical atheists"? How are practical atheists similar to pure atheists? How do they differ? Can a Christian be a practical atheist? How?

2. How do you explain the popularity of secular theology? What is secularism? Does it differ from materialism? How?

3. Can there be such a thing as a "Christian atheism"? Why or why not? Why has the death-of-God theology failed to retain its popularity?

4. How can we live in the world without in some sense being "secular"? Is all secular living bad? What about secular jobs and secular universities?

5. What is living "spiritually"? Should we distinguish between the secular and sacred in our lives? Or should we think of all of life as sacred and spiritual?

6. Why is it impossible to be self-sufficient and boastful about tomorrow? Why can't man achieve immortality apart from God?

7. According to James, life is a mist that soon vanishes. How should this reality affect our attitude toward how we live? toward possessions?

8. What did James mean by saying we ought to say, "If

the Lord wills, we shall live and we shall do this or that"? How do people misinterpret this admonition?

9. What are the dangers of the we-can-do-anything-we-please attitude? Is "doing your own thing" a Christian concept? Why or why not?

10. What are sins of omission (James 4:17)? How can sin be based on our knowledge of what is right or good? How can something not be sinful if we are ignorant about it and become sinful for us when we gain knowledge? Isn't this relativistic? Does this go contrary to absolute ethics?

11. Profit Now, Pay Later

"Come now, you rich, weep and howl for the miseries that are coming upon you. Your riches have rotted and your garments are moth-eaten. Your gold and silver have rusted, and their rust will be evidence against you and will eat your flesh like fire. You have laid up treasure for the last days. Behold, the wages of the laborers who mowed your fields, which you kept back by fraud, cry out; and the cries of the harvesters have reached the ears of the Lord of hosts. You have lived on the earth in luxury and in pleasure; you have fattened your hearts in a day of slaughter. You have condemned, you have killed the righteous man; he does not resist you" (James 5:1-6).

There's nothing intrinsically evil about money. Nor is there anything wrong in having a lot of it. A poor man can have as many hang-ups about money as a rich man. He can just as readily be trapped by envy as the rich. He can become a lover of money, so engrossed with gaining more that his obsession becomes sin. Against this kind of attitude toward money, whether in the heart of the rich or the poor, Paul says, "The love of money is the root of all evils" (I Tim. 6:10).

Before we get into the reasons why James has such harsh words of condemnation for the rich, let's establish a meaning for money. Why have money in the first place if it's such a dangerous commodity?

For most people in the world, money is probably the most sought after possession. Money is the most common means of exchange for the necessities of life. Each one of us exchanges some part of his life for material possessions—for money. A man or a woman will work in a factory, store, schoolroom, office, or other business place and literally give his present life (its abilities and time) for a certain amount of money. This is universally true whether a person lives in a democracy or a dictatorship, whether he is educated or uneducated, whether he is black or white, whether he is rich or poor. Money is the basic form of security around the world.

A person's income can be based on many things. It can be based on a certain fixed hourly rate, a fixed percentage of profits from sales, a percentage of gain on investments, a per job rate, or any other agreed method. No matter how it is calculated, it is based on a person's investment of his abilities and time. In the case of investments, the direct use of abilities and time involves others more than oneself.

Our money supplies the necessities of life—food, shelter, clothing, transportation, education, and leisure activities. Our money also supplies necessities of others through altruistic giving. Our work for the Lord is advanced by donating money to churches and other religious organizations. Beyond using it on ourselves, there are many opportunities to use our money in ways that benefit society.

For a Christian, money should have a servant role. As long as it is viewed from that perspective, we will use it fairly and wisely. If we use it to gain power over others who have less than we do, we become slaves to its power. Money must be a servant to help others as well as a servant to ourselves to live a good life that will honor God.

Some governmental leaders have the idea that money will solve all a country's ills. They propose massive expenditures for domestic and foreign programs as a way to solve the problems of humanity. But when these programs don't solve the problems, politicians rarely evaluate their actions. Rather, they devise new and bigger spending programs which are again proclaimed as the ultimate answers.

In politics as in business, money means power. Those with great wealth are able to control others and dominate the less wealthy. While showing a few inclinations for caring for the poor, they continue to amass money far beyond the amount they'll ever need to fulfill either their needs or their wants.

James's condemnation of the rich has to do with this attitude. He speaks to the rich who use their riches to dominate others and to those whose riches have been gained through cheating the poor (rather than from honest work and business practices). James talks about those who abused their employees by not paying them. He talked about those who "have laid up treasure for the last days," much like some rich people store it away for luxurious living and retirement years. To them James

98

cries out, "Weep and howl for the miseries that are coming upon you."

In a society that did not have governmental controls or regulations, the rich could set their own wage scales. This is illustrated in Christ's parable of the laborers who were sent into the harvest at different times of the day at an agreed wage, regardless of the hours worked. During New Testament times, even the Jewish people owned slaves. Slave owners never paid beyond subsistence wages. Slaves rarely amassed enough to purchase freedom. If a slave or a hired servant had little money to influence his dominant master, he had no leverage (as modern unions do) to improve his working conditions.

These conditions have existed throughout history, even in highly advanced and industrialized countries. Western society has done much to improve the lot of the poor and has broken some of the dominance of the rich. Antitrust and antimonopoly laws, unionization, and government regulation of wages and working conditions have a long way to go to alleviate massive hardship and poverty. Yet the poor are still with us and there is a tremendous need to bring about greater equity.

James tersely warns the rich about what the love of money can do to a person—both in this life and in the world to come. The picture he draws is not pleasant. Riches corrupt. Riches bring power. The rich soon misuse their power over the not-so-rich and the poor. The rich soon become insensitive to those around them. They devote their energies and time to gaining more possessions and power. They seek control over additional property and over the lives of more people so they can build greater economic empires, hire more people, and exercise even greater authority.

James said that the rich of his day got their gains by immoral means. They sent laborers into the harvest fields and then didn't pay the promised wages. They kept it back by fraud, he says. What worse sin could they commit? They denied the poor a decent livelihood. They made slaves of others. They caused people to starve. With greed they watched others suffer—simply to satisfy their own self-indulgent desires.

After expanding one's economic base, where does a man turn next but to luxuries and pleasures. James says that the rich "have lived on the earth in luxury and in pleasure." The rich can purchase all the personal comforts they desire. They can build homes that go far beyond what is necessary. They can entertain friends in luxurious partying.

Money can give the rich all the pleasures they desire. They can travel to any part of the world to enjoy its wonders. They can pay others to entertain them on theatrical stages or in sporting events. They can hire entertainers in private clubs or in their homes. Money can supply any self-indulgent desire they may dream up.

James warns the rich that their riches would rot and their garments would become moth-eaten. In ancient cultures, the rich purchased many precious stones, ointments, and exquisite garments from foreign nations. James warned them of the temporality of these material possessions. What value are they when they will soon rot or tarnish? They soon become worthless.

The rich, like many modern men, provided for their retirement and "laid up treasure for the last days" of their lives. But, according to James, riches provided no stability for those days. Though the rich thought they were well fixed for their retirement, they were on poor ground; for life does not guarantee that our earthly possessions can give absolute security. Disaster, inflation, taxes, and death can make security vanish.

Unfortunately, the rich are often deceived by their money. Their riches trick them. And the ultimate trick of their riches is to crowd out their dependence on God. They think money can maintain them throughout life. A man who trusts his money alone to take him through life leaves God outside. Jesus warned that a person cannot serve God and money. He will cling to the one or to the other. The person who clings to his money to solve life's problems doesn't cling to God.

What attitude should a person have toward money? Is it a sin to be rich? Not if a person has the right attitude toward his riches. If a person obtains and dispenses his money honestly and wisely in the light of God's truths, he will not become the victim of his riches. Money must always be a servant, not a master. The rich must not neglect the obligations of wealth, which include kindness and generosity toward the poor. His riches must not be obtained as a consequence of his injustice to the poor. He must consciously guard himself against becoming dull toward human needs. The rich man has a moral responsibility to society. He must answer positively the age-old question, "Am I my brother's keeper?" He must have a clear conscience before God as to how he uses what God has allowed him to have.

Lest we become self-satisfied and self-righteous by thinking, "That's not for me, that's for the rich," let's remember that most Westerners, especially Americans, have a higher standard of living than anyone on the earth. Today we are the rich of this world. We have an obligation to those around us. We cannot be smug about our wealth. We have to guard against living only for pleasure, luxury, and retirement. We must not allow ourselves to indulge in any self-gratification simply because we have the money to pay for it. We should live carefully as stewards of the abundance that God has graciously allowed us to possess. We must not forget the specially privileged place we have in America with all its economic and political power. Money, if properly used, can bring great blessing to people in need. Improperly used, wealth can curse many people through the creation of untold misery and injustice.

Christians have a tremendous opportunity to use their money for good, whether it be to advance missions, social services, or other charitable causes. We will not escape God's judgment if we have squandered our wealth on ourselves. But we will also be rewarded for using our money for advancing righteousness and justice. When we stand before God, we will either be judged for our greed or rewarded because in our generosity we have "done it unto the least of these." This is the kind of commitment that is desperately needed in our world today.

LET'S DISCUSS

1. Scripture has much to say about the evils of riches. Does this mean that Christians should strive to be poor? Is there any merit in being poor?
2. Why does James have so many bad things to say about the rich? Have the rich changed their character any since the time James wrote his letter?
3. Why do riches seem to be a deterrent to holy living? Why is it difficult for the rich to enter the kingdom of God?

4. Discuss some legitimate means for obtaining wealth. Do these methods guarantee justice toward poorer people? How?

5. How do you keep from loving money and the things it can purchase? How can a person determine when he has begun to love money? How can this be eliminated from one's life?

6. What are the dangers middle class people face concerning riches? How can they avoid these dangers? Can poor people be guilty of greed?

7. How can the church generate more money for its ministries? Is tithing a valid concept today? Is it a sin to give less than ten percent to the church? What is a reasonable amount to give to the Lord?

8. What are some of the joys of giving and sharing one's wealth with needy people? Why does giving produce a sense of satisfaction and joy? Why is it better to give than to receive?

9. How should Christians prepare for retirement? Does financial planning indicate a lack of faith? What about donating your estate to charity or to religious organizations or to your church? How much money should be left for heirs?

12. Why Be Patient?

" Be patient, therefore, brethren, until the coming of the Lord. Behold, the farmer waits for the precious fruit of the earth, being patient over it until it receives the early and the late rain. You also be patient. Establish your hearts, for the coming of the Lord is at hand. Do not grumble, brethren, against one another, that you may not be judged; behold, the Judge is standing at the doors. As an example of suffering and patience, brethren, take the prophets who spoke in the name of the Lord. Behold, we call those happy who were steadfast. You have heard of the steadfastness of Job, and you have seen the purpose of the Lord, how the Lord is compassionate and merciful" (James 5:7-11).

The red light turns to green. The driver in front of you is slow to start up and you are a little late for an appointment. How do you react? Do you start to honk your horn? Do you utter a few choice words about a slow-poke? Do you feel like pushing him? Or do you exercise one of the seemingly little used fruits of the Spirit—patience?

A child is told to clean his room. His mother wants it completed in an hour before she will take him to a baseball game. She watches him start slowly, get distracted by some toys or games, think of something to tell her that is more important than cleaning the room. She chafes with irritation. His room won't be cleaned in the allotted time. The boy does not work according to her specifications. She gets angry and begins to scold him. He pouts and accomplishes less. She punishes him with a couple of slaps. After it is all over, the mother wonders why she doesn't have the ability to be patient with her son. Why is patience so difficult even in the ordinary circumstances of life?

Despite our ever-increasing speed for getting things done and getting from one place to the other, our speeded up living has done little to improve human relations. In fact, our impatience seems to grow worse in spite of our numerous time-saving devices. We want them so we'll have more time to do what we desire. Unfortunately, we simply use our time in more speedy, frustrating activities. Why don't these inventions help us become patient? The patience that James talks about in this chapter goes beyond putting up with the frustrations of our mechanized society and irritations caused by traffic tie-ups. It goes beyond mere things to people. To deal only with our relationship to things does not solve the problem of impatience. The personal agony of suffering in patience is not merely a physical experience. It taxes both the mind and the spirit. By expressing patience toward people, we express love. The patience James talked about demands love. And when we love, we must suffer not only pain but waiting by "forbearing one another . . . forgiving each other" (Col. 3:13). In our Lord's personal life, patience never seemed to take conscious effort.

This does not mean that patience is passive. While it is not something we think about consciously, nevertheless it is a fruit of the Spirit that we express actively. We do not go around saying, "I am going to be patient today." We simply act patiently. In other words, when it is a natural, unconscious attitude, it is more readily practiced. Patience is not something we can drum up by telling ourselves to be patient. It is a result of daily contact with God through prayer and by understanding and accepting His will for us.

James beautifully illustrates the ideal of patience by reference to a farmer. The farmer first works diligently preparing the soil for seeding. He then plants the seed, making sure this is accomplished at the right time of the year. In Palestine this was important because of the spacing of the rainy seasons. They came only twice during the growing season. The farmer had to get the seed into the soil before the first rain to give the seed adequate moisture for sprouting and growth.

The farmer did not sit on his hands on a stump at the edge of the field once the seed was planted. He didn't stay there waiting for the plants to pop up through the surface. He went about doing his necessary work—with the confidence that the seed would grow. At the appropriate times, he cultivated the field to eliminate weeds and to preserve the precious moisture. With the hope that it would rain before the crops ripened, he continued his work without fretting.

The farmer had seen many plantings and harvestings;

therefore he could go about his tasks calmly and confidently, methodically preparing for the time of harvesting. He trusted that it would rain, that the crops would ripen, and that he would enjoy a harvest in due season. Impatience with the crop as it developed would have been foolishness. Pacing back and forth at the edge of the field would do absolutely nothing to speed the ripening process. He had learned through previous experience that the best way to operate was to work while he waited. The harvest would come.

Life hasn't changed on this score throughout the centuries. Farmers still face seedtime and harvest. They still must do a considerable amount of work while the crops are growing and ripening.

The example is quite clear: we must go about our business and wait patiently for our goals to come to fruition. We must not pace at life's field edges, so to speak. That would be a foolish waste of energy. Without being fatalistic we can agree with Manford Gutzke when he proclaimed, "Everything moves to a showdown." Ours is not to fret about this fact or to fret about the slowness of the movement. Ours is to know where we fit into the movement and to trust God to work through us until the final harvest.

This truth of the coming showdown is presented in several parables Jesus told. The parable of the sower and the seed (Matt. 13:3-9) dittos what James has presented. The parable of the wheat and the tares shows the separation of the good and evil at harvest time (Matt. 13:24-30). The parable of the talents (Matt. 25:14-30) demonstrates the showdown of rewards when the master demands an accounting for every man. The parable of the ten virgins (Matt. 25:1-13) also deals with this final accounting. The parable of the sheep and the goats (Matt. 25:31-46) is another that shows the separation of the good and evil.

We are not called to sit around and wait for things to happen. That isn't true patience; that's procrastination. Patience involves work as well as waiting. It involves activity, not a cessation of involvement. It involves endurance, not simply passive acceptance of circumstances.

Christians are challenged to endure to the end (Matt. 10:22; Mark 13:13). This means going all the way in attempting to reach the final line. Paul gives the example of athletes in a foot race. They all run the entire race even though only one is the victor. The others do not stop running when they see one man cross the finish line. They persevere to the finish even though they do not win a prize.

The prophets were often called upon to endure rejection and physical suffering (James 5:10). The prophet Isaiah was told by the Lord right at the beginning of his sixty-year ministry that the people of Israel would not listen to his message. But that gave him no excuse to give up proclaiming the message of Jehovah.

Jeremiah was persecuted by those to whom God had sent him. They didn't appreciate his clear warnings of impending doom, with the result that his sensitive and warm-hearted personality endured continual abuses. And though he was often persecuted and ridiculed, he continued to fulfill his calling. He was compelled to go on by a sense of divine urgency. Not even prison, stocks, or torture could dampen his persistent faithfulness to God.

Job has become the byword for patience in our Western civilization. People speak of the "patience of Job" (James 5:11) yet don't even know the circumstances of his life or where to find the full details. They simply utter this phrase to describe someone who has great patience. A close examination of Job's life will indicate that he didn't always take his suffering comfortably and easily. He felt pain and cried out. The patience he displayed was wrapped up in his relationship to God. He knew how to wait for the Lord and he maintained his integrity throughout his trials. And though he lost patience with his so-called comforters, he did not deny God. He "did not sin with his lips" (Job 2:10) or charge God with wrong (Job 1:22). When his wife told him to curse God and die, he told her that she was speaking foolishness. Though he could not understand the reason for his sufferings, he had the integrity to endure with patience. He believed, though he could not understand.

James teaches us not to be impatient with God. We are to be patient "until the coming of the Lord" (5:7). should not expect Him to judge quickly just because we desire release from frustration or pressure. We must leave judgment in His hands, to be worked according to His timetable. Nor should we assume the role of a judge to bring quick punishment upon others. The temptation to lose patience often leads to the sins of vindictiveness and despair.

So how do we become patient? Do we stoically put up with our circumstances? Do we just grin and bear it? No! On the contrary, we must learn the secret of combining obedience with waiting. We are strengthened by waiting upon the Lord—and His strength will help us face the upsetting conflicts of life.

Those who try to be patient by their own powers usually do not obtain their goals. Patience is one of the fruits of the Spirit that is a byproduct of obedience rather than a direct endowment. It comes as a result of the Holy Spirit's control in a person's life. Rather than being a directly sought spiritual virtue, patience is an indirect benefit to the Christian. As the fruit of the Spirit is developed, so will patience grow. Real patience comes when the powerful love of Christ is active in our lives. As we express love, patience develops. As one commits himself to the Lord, patience grows within. The person develops and patience expresses itself through kindness, love, and a concern for others.

LET'S DISCUSS

1. How do you define patience? What Scripture verses support your view? Name and describe some biblical examples of patience.
2. Why does it seem so difficult to be patient? Does our fast-moving culture have anything to do with it? Explain.
3. Why is it easy to become critical and judgmental when we are impatient? How can this be overcome?
4. Describe how patience is expressed or manifested. How is this related to waiting on the Lord? What does it mean to wait on the Lord? Does waiting mean inactivity?
5. Romans 2:4 and I Peter 3:20 speak of God's patience. Does this mean that He sometimes overlooks man's sin? Why doesn't He inflict speedy punishment upon sinners?
6. How do you show patience in tense and difficult situations? Give some examples and discuss how the outcome was helped by your patient attitude.

7. Are there ways to relieve tensions and frustrations that prompt impatience? What part should psychology play? Where does Christ fit into the process? Where does the Holy Spirit fit in?

8. Can you give examples of times when impatience could be acceptable and valuable? Are there any biblical situations to support this?

9. Why should we not grumble against one another? In what sense is grumbling against our brothers making unwarranted judgments? Who is our judge?

10. How can understanding the purpose of the Lord help us to be more patient? How can we gain knowledge of God's purposes? Does James give us an answer?

13. Does God Heal Today ?

"Is any one among you suffering? Let him pray. Is any cheerful? Let him sing praise. Is any among you sick? Let him call for the elders of the church, and let them pray over him, anointing him with oil in the name of the Lord; and the prayer of faith will save the sick man, and the Lord will raise him up; and if he has committed sins, he will be forgiven. Therefore confess your sins to one another, and pray for one another, that you may be healed. The prayer of a righteous man has great power in its effects. Elijah was a man of like nature with ourselves and he prayed fervently that it might not rain, and for three years and six months it did not rain on the earth. Then he prayed again and the heaven gave rain, and the earth brought forth its fruit.

"My brethren, if any one among you wanders from the truth and some one brings him back, let him know that whoever brings back a sinner from the error of his way will save his

soul from death and will cover a multitude of sin" (James 5:13-20).

People throughout history have attributed unexplained healings to supernatural powers. Many people have claimed to have power to perform miraculous healings. The Roman Catholic Church at Lourdes, France, has been a center of "miracles" allegedly performed through the influence of the Virgin Mary. Christian Scientists claim healing through acceptance of their doctrine of the nonexistence of disease and evil. Faith healers have claimed to have received a special gift from God. Revival of the charismatic movement has brought a new emphasis on the doctrine of divine healing. The Jesus Movement has also put stress upon the "gift" of healing. So the controversy as to whether "divine healing" is a ministry of the church continues.

There is no question that the Bible teaches that God miraculously worked within the lives of men to heal their diseases. Jesus performed many miracles of healing (Matt. 9:20-22; Matt. 9:2-7; Luke 4:46-54). Matthew 10:1 tells us that Jesus gave the power of healing to the disciples. Paul further states this in I Corinthians 12:28 where he lists—among other gifts given to those in the church—"healers" as those appointed by God (I Cor. 12:9, 28, 30). Paul makes it quite clear that not every person was healed because prayers were made for healing. In his own case he says, "Three times I besought the Lord about this, that it should leave me; but he said to me, 'My grace is sufficient for you, for my power is made perfect in weakness' " (II Cor. 12:8, 9).

One must ask, Does healing today differ from New Testament healing? Can we simply pray, expecting God to give instantaneous cures similar to many that are recorded in the Bible? Would it be proper to inject the idea that "laying on of hands" possibly could include the ministry of doctors today? Was healing a New Testament era phenomenon or something discontinued as the church became established in the world?

Should we not also be aware of the culture in which the New Testament church developed? During that era, doctors knew little more than how to use herb medicines. Along with their limited knowledge was the expense involved—something out of the reach of most of the poor people. The Christian emphasis on "bearing one another's burdens" would draw people to have considerable interest in the sick, much as they were also instructed by James to have interest in the orphans and widows (1:27). This was a part of their "genuine religion."

Charismatic groups have made this passage a proof text for what has become known as "faith healing." It has also been used as the basis of the Roman Catholic doctrine of extreme unction and the confessional. The Roman Catholic Church has interpreted the term "elders" to be "priests." So, when one is unable to help himself because of sickness or if one has a sickness that is unto death, the priest prays over the dying person. Of course, even casual reading of these verses reveals that the reference isn't necessarily to a dying person.

It is very important that we notice that James tells the sick to call the elders of the church—the leaders of the church—to come and pray. He makes no reference to those who have the gift of healing as described by Paul. Surely this gift was present in the church in James' time before Paul wrote his Letter to the Corinthians. Why was the healer left out? Why did James give this specific instruction to call the leaders? Was it because James had some particular practice in mind and a particular result that he was proclaiming would happen in the sick man's life?

Another point of controversy in this passage is in the anointing of the sick with oil by the elders. What significance did this have? Was it medicinal or symbolic? Did it have a symbolic significance such as the anointing of the feet of Jesus by Mary? If the anointing with oil was a literal, physical application to bring about healing, then the type of sickness would have been limited to something primarily muscular. If it was symbolic, it would have a deeper meaning—a physical healing of something inward.

One of the dangers in interpreting a passage such as this is to apply our preconceived ideas about how God works. Those of the dispensational persuasion say that the age of miracles is past. Those with charismatic beliefs say that we are seeing a revival of divine healing through specially chosen people. Since this passage does not spell out every fine point, we cannot be dogmatic; yet we must stay within the limitations of what is presented. Another question of interest is whether the sickness was totally physical, or whether James was referring to the spiritually weak as well.

It is interesting to note that the two words used for "sick" in this text are different. In verse 14, the word is the same as used for physical illness in Matthew 10:8 and other New Testament passages. In verse 15, the word for "sick" means "fatigued" and could be interpreted to apply to a spiritual condition as well as a physical condition. Taken together, it might be that both the physical and the spiritual conditions would be included in the prayer of the elders who prayed and anointed the sick with oil in the name of the Lord.

An important formula, according to James, in the healing procedure is that the anointing and the prayer be "in the name of the Lord." When the seventy disciples returned from their mission, they joyfully reported to Jesus that the demons were subjected to them "in your name" (Luke 10:17). Peter healed the lame man at the Beautiful Gate in the "name of the Lord" (Acts 3:6), and the slave girl was healed by Paul in "the name of the Lord." The phrase "in the name of the Lord" is most likely a reference to the authority and power of Jesus Christ. The miracle taking place had to do with the power of God, not with the power of the individual making the pronouncement of healing.

James said that "the prayer of faith will save the sick man." This is presumed to be the prayer by the elders and is in reference to the healing of the sick. Some have suggested that it possibly could have been the prayer of the sick man himself, made in relationship to the condition of his soul, because of the words "if he has committed sins, he will be forgiven." There was no need for forgiveness for the sickness itself, but for sins—even those which might have caused his sickness.

At times sickness has its origin in sin (Mark 2:5-12). But Jesus denied emphatically that sickness is always caused by sin (John 9:3; Luke 13:1-5). James does not necessarily say that sin is the cause of the sickness, but he recognized that it might be a possibility. He says "if," which makes it plain that there is not an automatic connection. But James is clear in pronouncing that "the Lord will raise him up." The miracle of healing is totally the work of the Lord.

It is not mere prayer that will alter the condition of the sick, but the *prayer of faith*. There are numerous references in the New Testament to show the connection between healing and faith (Matt. 8:8; Mark 2:5; 7:29; 9:24). Faith does not always have to be present in the person being healed. It can be the faith of others. James' reference therefore could be either to the faith of the elders or the faith of the sick person.

It also seems plain from the text that those who come to pray for the sick ought to be concerned not only for his bodily needs, but also for his spiritual condition. And as they show that concern, they are able to share needs that go beyond one's physical condition. It is possible to become so absorbed in the healing aspect of this text that we fail to see the other concern in the healing relationship. James teaches that Christians ought to confess their sins one to another, and pray for one another, that they may be healed. While the Roman Catholic Church has made this to be a reference to their concept of confession to a priest, evangelicals have minimized the value of public confession.

The old adage said, "Confession is good for the soul." There are some sins that perhaps should be mentioned only in a private devotional session with the Lord, but there are sins common among all Christians that ought to be more openly confessed. No one is harmed by confessing his weaknesses and faults to those who are mature in the faith and who seek to be of mutual help.

To be afraid to confess sins to one another indicates a certain falseness of spirit, a pride that hinders one from having a healing relationship with others within the community of faith. To hide behind a facade of individ-

117

uality or private devotional orientation, to be afraid to expose our souls to others, to fear that we might be overemotional—all these indicate a lack of humility and real concern to be all that God would have us be in transparency of spirit toward other believers. Such fears are simply hiding behind a mask of spirituality and respectability.

Sensitivity training has come under attack by many Christians because it seems to expose an individual more than is necessary. Perhaps some attempts and experiences at sensitivity training have been abusive to the individual and have caused greater psychological problems than they have healed. However, this does not change the fact that an open and honest expression of one's feelings to another person can have tremendous therapeutic effect. The proper kind of group therapy, with a Christian understanding of the human personality and a Christian answer to human needs, can have a healing effect. Confession of sins can play this role within the guilt-ridden person whose fundamental need is to get outside of himself and feel the warmth within the Christian community.

James goes on to emphasize the power of prayer. He said that "the prayer of a righteous man has great power in its effects" (5:16); and he reminds the reader of Elijah, a man who performed miracles, a man highly respected by the Jewish people to whom James had specifically pointed his letter, and who through prayer caused drought in the land of Israel for three and a half years. James also points out that it was through Elijah's prayer that rain came to bring forth fruit in the land (vv. 17, 18).

Throughout our study of this passage, we must not

forget that God works through men—men like Elijah who was "a man of like nature with ourselves." Even though Elijah stood out in the memory of James' readers, James was quick to point out that Elijah was the same as they were—a man. An examination of I Kings 19 will show exactly how human Elijah really was. All men have access to God; and when they pray fervently and sincerely, God will cause mighty things to happen.

James closes his book with encouragement to those who help a person return to the truth after straying (5:19, 20). From the context, we might assume that the conversion was effected in large part through the power of prayer.

There has always been controversy over verse 20. Does the return of the erring sinner save the sinner's soul from death or does it save the soul of the person responsible for his return? If the reference is to the returning sinner, the last phrase of the book—"and will cover a multitude of sins"—is a natural conclusion; for through an erring person's conversion his sins would be covered by the blood of Christ.

No matter how we interpret this entire passage we are encouraged by James' emphasis on the efficacy of prayer, whether made by the suffering individual (v. 13) or by the leaders of the church (v. 14), by the sick (v. 15) or the righteous man (v. 16), or by the great prophet (vv. 17, 18). Rather than arguing about the meaning of prayer and its power, what we really need is to pray more effectively.

LET'S DISCUSS

1. Jesus and His apostles healed the sick. Were there

particular kinds of diseases and sicknesses that they healed? Explain. Did their miracles have common elements? What were the purposes of their healing?

2. The apostle Paul said that healing was a gift. What is the nature of this gift? Is this still a valid gift within the church? Is there any evidence that it is not?

3. Why did James teach that the elders of the church ought to be called to pray over the sick? Was this in absence of an individual with the gift of healing? Did the elders possess the gift?

4. Was the anointing of oil a medicinal or symbolic act? How was oil used in Old and New Testament times as a healing agent? Is it used so today?

5. Is there a relationship between sin and disease? Does all disease indicate that a person has committed sins?

6. What is the value of "confessing your sins to one another"? Is this a basis for confession to a priest or minister? What are the dangers of public confession of sins? Should certain sins be confessed only to God?

7. Discuss the relationship between modern "faith healing" and the New Testament teaching on healing.

8. What criteria can we use today to evaluate the claims of miraculous healing? What relationship does the medical profession have to this?

9. Is skepticism regarding faith healing an evidence of a lack of faith? Why do so many Christians doubt the efficacy of modern healers? Would you pray for divine healing for yourself or for your loved ones?